My Beggar's
PURSE

Wisdom for Life
Series of Women's Devotional Books

God's Pitcher by Gloria Baird

My Bucket of Sand by Sheila Jones

My Beggar's Purse by Linda Brumley

My Beggar's
PURSE

And Other Spiritual Thoughts

Linda Brumley

www.dpibooks.org

My Beggar's Purse
©2010 by DPI Books
5016 Spedale Court #331
Spring Hill, TN 37174

Printed in the United States of America

Cover Design: Brian Branch
Front Cover Photo: ©istockphotos/Knorre
Interior Design: Thais Gloor

ISBN: 978-1-57782-256-1

To the ten wonderful people who, through their
equally wonderful parents (my four children),
share some portions of my DNA:
Sara, Becca, Tucker, Jason, Tyler,
Michael, Hunter, Emma, Cole and Sutton.
I pray you will also always share my love
for God and his inerrant word.

CONTENTS

Acknowledgments..9
Wisdom for Life 11

1. My Beggar's Purse 13
2. Identity 20
3. Mastectomy: Take One 25
4. Faith's Basis...33
5. Character and Change 39
6. Prayer 46
7. Learning Obedience 52
8. Valuable in God's Sight 61
9. Resembling Daddy 66
10. A Quiet Spirit 70
11. Invisible Blessings 75
12. Accepting Help 80
13. Perspective 87
14. Joy and Happiness 91
15. Focus and Priorities 97
16. Reasoning with God 102
17. Staying Awake..105
18. One Day at a Time 112
19. Running on Empty 119
20. Generational Sins 125
21. Judging God 132
22. Disputes 141

23. Submission 147
24. Theme Songs 152

Thoughts from the Author 160

OTHER WRITINGS

Godly Emotions 163
Eve: The Great Deception 174
Joanna: A Gutsy Follower 182

Acknowledgments

I'd like to thank my friend and confidant, Sheila Jones, whose editing expertise has kept me from making a fool of myself. (Dear reader, if you feel I have made a fool of myself anyway, please blame Sheila, not me!)

And thanks to Ron who, in our 50th year of marriage, remains my best counselor, editor, friend, lover and source of laughter on this earth. God has used him repeatedly to add wisdom and perspective to my beggar's purse.

WISDOM FOR LIFE
Devotional Series

In the Wisdom for Life devotional series, older women with years of life experience and biblical insight share truths that have helped them and others through the years.

If you sometimes wish you could just sit down at the table across from a spiritual mom and hear some of the important things she has learned in her life, this is your chance.

Gloria Baird wrote the first volume, entitled *God's Pitcher,* and Sheila Jones wrote the second volume, *My Bucket of Sand.* In this volume, *My Beggar's Purse,* you will experience the wit, humility and spiritual depth of Linda Brumley. In the months to come there will be more volumes, more wisdom, more "table talks" with women who have much to share.

Each volume will be unique because each woman, like you, is one of a kind.

We pray that as you read, you will be encouraged and will gain "wisdom for life."

> Likewise, teach the older women to be reverent in
> the way they live, not to be slanderers or addicted to

much wine, but to teach what is good. Then they can train the younger women to love their husbands and children, to be self-controlled and pure, to be busy at home, to be kind, and to be subject to their husbands, so that no one will malign the word of God. (Titus 2:3–5)

1

My Beggar's Purse

On a visit one day to a wonderful dim sum restaurant, I was served a delicacy called a "beggar's purse." Its name is derived from its shape: a wonton wrapper gathered up in a tidy bundle around a dollop of savory ground meat, tied with a chive and steamed to perfection. While the subtle flavors delighted my palate, the shape and the name captured my imagination.

I thought of street beggars in China, all their earthly belongings knotted into a piece of cloth and a smaller version becoming a makeshift wallet in which to place the coins of benevolent passers-by.

Then I thought of how that mirrored me as I go to God. I am a beggar before God—in prayer as I seek his blessings in my life, and in my study of the Word as I store its treasures in my heart. I come to my Father utterly incapable of supplying my own needs without his generous provision. In his word I find wisdom, direction, motivation, security and meaningful purpose in life. In prayer, I find a love relationship, hope, release and freedom from guilt.

I go to God, spreading my beggar's purse open before him and waiting for him to fill it with the things I will need to make it through the day. He has never failed me, although I have failed him.

While I am absolutely sure that prayer and Bible study are the sustenance of the Christian life, and that my need for God is a constant factor, it is life circumstances that put me emotionally in touch or out of touch with my soul's desperation. I once believed that I would reach a level of spiritual maturity that would transcend life's busyness and distractions and my own hyperactive nature. I'm still waiting for that patient steadfastness with a measure of personal disappointment.

Still, when I'm facing a tough decision, it is the Bible and prayer (and the advice of godly friends) that set my course. I have never encountered a life circumstance that is not effectively addressed in the Bible. God has, indeed, given us "everything we need for life and godliness" (2 Peter 1:3). When I'm discouraged or fearful, it is the comfort of prayer and the direction of God's word that bring peace and perspective (Matthew 11:28). When I'm happily curious and searching the Scriptures for some new understanding to ground me, I'm thrilled by the practicality of this living Word (Hebrews 4:12).

I love reading Psalm 119 and measuring my current

love for the Word against David's. I always come up short of that man after God's own heart (1 Samuel 13:14), but he inspires me to have that mark on the wall as a measure for my own enthusiasm for the precepts of God.

You might think with all this professed conviction that I'd never miss a day of Bible study. Not so. I had a friend who set as a New Year's resolution the goal of not missing a single day of reading the Bible. She did it. There are probably others who have never missed a day in the Word in years and find it unthinkable to do otherwise. But I miss a day now and then. This, in spite of my awe that so brief a tome contains the entire will of God!

I'm puzzled by college graduates who have read several books (of infinitely lesser value) in a single semester for the sake of passing a class, yet who claim not to have time to read the entire Bible.

Prayer is another thing. I may miss a good, long morning prayer once in a while, but the little comments and requests I send in God's direction throughout the day are a way of life for me now. Still, I know those times when I have a real conversation with God and pour out my heart to him are the true grounding connections in my relationship with him.

I have experienced a few periods of life when I felt buried under the weight of sorrow or fear. While these were the times I most needed connection with God, they were also the ones in which I found it most challenging to focus. Those were the times when I had to write out my prayers just to be able to concentrate and remember that I had, indeed, prayed that day. Those written prayers anchored me and gave me confidence that a faithful God had heard me and was at work crafting the perfect response to my perceived needs. I've sometimes spread those written prayers before God the way Hezekiah did with Sennacherib's letter and asked God to look at it with me and deliver me (2 Kings 19:14–19).

One of these challenging times in my life happened several years ago. Our youngest son passed out while on a morning walk and was hospitalized for eleven days while doctors tried to determine the cause of abdominal pain so severe they could find no remedy. An uncertain diagnosis left them unable to provide much help beyond strong painkillers.

He was frightened and depressed and on a downward cycle spiritually. My own fear was consuming and left me numb when I tried to pray. I couldn't seem to voice my requests to God. Instead, I filled a journal with prayers. Matt finally learned to manage his health with a rigid diet which he has courageously followed, and he accepted the help he needed to get back on track with his relationship with God.

During some of these challenging times, I've also felt unable to concentrate on reading the Bible, so I have resorted to reading it aloud. Getting two of my senses involved in comprehension seems to help me. I try to read with lots of appropriate inflection. Particularly challenging times are not the best times for me to read Leviticus or Revelation. Still, no matter my state of mind, I always come away with treasures.

Prayer and Scripture: the priceless currency in my beggar's purse!

Occasionally, I find surprises when I open my beggar's purse in a crisis. I find God has equipped me with a new strength of character to meet the current trial. I find he's extended my ability to persevere or gifted me with hope. I've been happily surprised to find he's forged his full armor (Ephesians 6:10–18) to a greater tensile strength than I'd have ever noticed if I had not needed to go into battle.

When life's troubles blindside you, as they most often do, you can feel unprepared and even disoriented as you stumble around, trying to get your bearings to focus on a spiritual and emotional course to see you through. I can't think of a single trial that I went into feeling fully prepared. Instead, I have felt initially frenzied and frightened, rummaging through my beggar's purse looking for the resources that will equip me to face the current crisis: "Where's that sword—that sword of the Spirit? I know it was right here! Snap! I should have sharpened it! Is there any patience stored in here somewhere? I never seem to have enough perseverance on hand! Hope—I get a glimpse of it and when I reach for it, it seems to have moved just out of reach behind some nasty negative obstruction."

But usually, in the end, I'm able to pull together just the right equipment that God has supplied to sustain me.

Years ago, I volunteered to care for an elderly friend who had just been released from the hospital. She was a week or two from being able to take care of herself and had no family able to provide for her.

We gave her our guest room, just off our living room. Unfortunately, she found herself to be more comfortable on our living room sofa. I didn't want an invalid in our living room, but I knew it wasn't forever and her comfort was more important than my sense of the appropriate. I searched around in my beggar's purse for the love and patience to be at peace with her needs. I barely found enough.

Her age and the condition for which she had been hospitalized made walking a slow and halting process. Our four children were still young, and I already felt stretched with meeting their needs, but found I had temporarily added another "toddler" to my brood. I searched around in my purse for humor.

The final stretch for me was that she had limited control over her bowels, and I found myself regularly spot-cleaning the bathroom floor and sometimes the gold shag carpet in the living room. This put me at the end of my resources. It was more than I'd signed on for when I originally offered to bring my friend home. I opened wide my beggar's purse as I went to my Father, confessing my weary self-pity and begging for the ability to sweetly fulfill my promise to assist with her recovery.

I found God had put within me a pretty good spiritual imagination. Recalling Jesus' promise in Matthew 25 that when we serve others, he receives it as service rendered personally to him, I became armed with a new resolve. On my hands and knees scrubbing my soiled carpet, I pretended I was cleaning up after Jesus. It gave me the most amazing joy! I felt humbled and honored to have this great privilege of serving my Lord. Who knew that make-believe was a gift of the Spirit?

I love being a beggar at the feet of a loving and generous God.

2

IDENTITY

In Western culture, women search for or try to create their own persona. We base our identities on our appearance or our accomplishments or our heritage or our relationships or any combination of the four, trying to "find ourselves." We try to be "true to ourselves." We try to be "authentic."

In my early twenties, I was a college student, the wife of a young school teacher and a church-goer. I had a different persona for each of these backdrops. On campus, I sought connection with my fellow students as ardently as I had in high school. I tried to be smart—competitively smart—I tried to be funny and hip and flirty (never mind that I was married).

I hated being with my husband's colleagues. They seemed so mature and intellectual. I felt young and foolish. I should have just felt humble and interested, but I was trying to fit in by impressing a crowd with whom I had little in common. Some of the women teachers in his district played bridge monthly and invited me to join them. I didn't know how to play bridge. I went anyway. I found them mostly gossiping (I had nothing to contribute but a willing ear), and smoking (I didn't smoke, but would not have dreamed of admitting it), so I accepted the offered cylinders and lit them and didn't inhale—honest! I can't imagine how stupid I must have looked.

Then I dropped out of college during my first pregnancy and added the element of motherhood to my search for self. I wanted to prove that I was the perfect wife and mother. Unfortunately, my efforts at proving myself insulated me from seeking advice because, after all, I was trying to demonstrate that I already knew everything. Thus my house and my children just became show pieces designed to make me look good.

At church I dressed appropriately, sang appropriately, made appropriate comments in Sunday school class, and volunteered appropriately to help with the weekly bulletin. I liked this persona better than the other ones, but didn't see the hypocrisy dominating my life.

Naturally, none of this was fulfilling. I found myself lying awake in tears one night, trying to decide which of these masks was the real me. I realized I was a prisoner of my efforts to be what I thought others wanted me to be. That night I decided to start reading the Bible to see if I could figure out who God wanted me to be. I thought that if I could be sure I was pleasing God, maybe I would not care so much that I seemed unable to please anyone else.

The first thing I learned was that I couldn't please God—not on my own, anyway! His standard is perfection, and it was way too late for that; too much sin already sullied my history. I found God's description of me in Romans 3:10–12:

> "There is no one righteous, not even one;
>   there is no one who understands, no one who
>   seeks God.
> All have turned away,
>   they have together become worthless;
> there is no one who does good, not even one."

Then I learned that he loved me anyway (John 3:16), had provided a way to see me as perfect (Hebrews 10:14), and was offering me the greatest treasure in the universe—a relationship with him (2 Corinthians 5:18–19). While this information thrilled me and I wanted to avail myself of these marvelous blessings, that "perfect" business was a tough concept.

I know a lot of women who experience the same struggle. In spite of all the trouble God has gone to in the Bible to explain our fallen state, we still feel we need to somehow do something to deserve salvation. We try to be perfect Christians and perfect wives and perfect mothers, and we get defensive if anyone points out that we are not, all the while beating ourselves up because we *know* we are not. It is such an exhausting contradiction.

Don't get me wrong—aiming for perfection is the right thing to do (2 Corinthians 13:11), but *claiming* it is a lie (1 John 1:8–9), and going around in a constant state of angst because we are imperfect is a miserable way to live. It is not what God had in mind.

God doesn't want us to be comfortable sinning, but he does want us to be comfortable with the fact that we are sinners. I think we work so hard to *be* the treasure instead of being entrusted with the treasure:

> But we have this treasure in jars of clay to show that this all-surpassing power is from God and not from us. (2 Corinthians 4:7)

We are jars of clay—the muddy-colored, misshapen kind; not the elegantly glazed, hand-painted, porcelain kind. And God has chosen to fill us with a treasure:

> For God, who said, "Let light shine out of darkness," made his light shine in our hearts to give us the light of the knowledge of the glory of God in the face of Christ. (2 Corinthians 4:6)

So, this is my identity. I am a jar of clay. My job is not to "find myself," but to die to myself (Luke 9:23–26). At what cost? Just clay. But I'm so excited that God can use me anyway! It is because of the treasure within—the knowledge of the plan of God for the salvation of all mankind—that my life has meaning and glory.

Replacing our self-concepts, which have been shaped by the accumulated shame and failures of our lives, happens when we let God fill our beggar's purses with his view of us—brand new and holy, stamped with his seal of approval (2 Corinthians 5:16–19). The Bible is full of wonderful assurances about how God sees us. They are hard to believe for those of us prone to self-recrimination, but they are jewels to treasure and to accept as truth, causing us to reject the accusatory lies with which Satan tries to demean us. This is why we need our beggar's purses from which we can pull out the sacred truths that defeat our inner voices.

3

Mastectomy: Take One

I was fifty-two years old and living in Chicago the first time I was diagnosed with breast cancer. I've never been one to worry about my health, so I was completely blindsided and totally unprepared emotionally. In fact, in the early 1980s I had worked for a biochemist who had volumes of printed research on breast cancer. One of my tasks was to read, summarize and catalog all his articles. I convinced myself that I fit none of the predictors for breast cancer and assured myself it was definitely not in my future.

Surprise! I've decided *surprise* is a horribly disruptive experience unless it is a good surprise. Emotionally, I felt I was free-falling and desperately looking for a cord to pull on a parachute that would let me down safely and gently. I found several elements that made my landing easier.

This is where I began rummaging around in my beggar's purse for the coping mechanisms to see me through this trial. Initially, I wasn't sure what I might find in there to help me conquer my fears and quell the approaching hysteria.

First, I reviewed foundational beliefs in my heart. I anchored myself in the trust that (1) I would not be given more than I could bear (1 Corinthians 10:13), (2) All things work together for the good of those who love the Lord (Romans 8:28), and (3) There is reason to rejoice in every trial because of the work God does in my character as I persevere through it (James 1:2–4). I had to return to these convictions again and again as each day brought new fearful and/or painful experiences and frustrating delays.

For me, one of the hardest things about cancer is the time you have to spend in limbo while you await biopsy results, additional testing, a definitive prognosis and a protocol for treatment. Limbo is a hard place to live for someone who likes to feel prepared for what might lie ahead. Surrendering to the bleak unknown and leaving your future in God's hands is an enormous spiritual exercise. It is rarely accomplished in a day, and it is rarely permanent. It usually has to be renewed with each new threat or discouragement that assaults your peace of mind.

Relaxing into the knowledge that someone was going to cut off my left breast was a process. I remember standing naked in front of a full length mirror and asking myself which appendage I would rather a surgeon remove: a hand, an ear, a foot, a breast? A breast, for sure! This was a helpful exercise.

I sat on a kitchen stool one afternoon and suddenly flashed to a scene from *Alice in Wonderland* where the Queen of Hearts orders Alice's decapitation. "Off with her breast," I cried! And then I retreated immediately to watch the Disney video, replacing in my mind's eye my breast surgeon for the evil Queen of Hearts, and the rest of the doctors and radiology techs and other medical professionals for the queen's army in hot pursuit of poor little me. It was an inescapable diagnosis with an equally inescapable solution (short of an unwise rebellion on my part). I was running emotionally, but there was no outrunning the mandate of medical science

That first day when leaving the oncological surgeon's office, I was given a stack of pamphlets addressing the various aspects of breast cancer. I know these are tremendously helpful and serve to answer the myriad questions you can't possibly think to ask in an office appointment. Even so, it can feel like a bit of a brush off by the doctor, as if she's saying, "Read this stuff and don't bother me."

On the top of the stack was one called "Why Me?" I was struck by this title because it was a question I had not been tempted to ask. Pondering my omission of this natural query, I landed on this answer: "Why me?" has a whole different meaning for me because of my faith in God. I found within my beggar's purse the belief that while God does not cause the misfortunes in our lives, he does allow them and has plans to use them for good. So my take on this was to be on the lookout for the great reasons God trusted me to go on this journey.

Maybe he wanted me to meet someone whom I would otherwise never encounter. Maybe he had lessons for me to learn that I could not learn any other way. Maybe he had people in my future who would need my empathy from firsthand experience. Maybe he wanted me to show someone what it looks like to trust God. Maybe he wanted to deepen my spiritual friendships through my new need for a support system. Maybe he wanted to humble me with a deeper understanding of my own mortality and vulnerability.

Perhaps God's purposes would remain a mystery, but these possibilities kept me alert to opportunities to share my faith and kept hope alive in my heart.

The time between diagnosis and surgery stretched from May to the end of July. I was bouncing between clinics and tests, trying to coordinate different doctors' schedules to align with an available operating room. This delay was not life-threatening, and my doctors assured me I had six months before they would consider a further delay a problem. Still, for me, the wait was emotionally draining since I have a strong "let's get it over with" inclination once I begin to anticipate suffering. A wimp, I consider any surgery to equal suffering.

One of my biggest fears was how my husband would react to my altered image. I discovered that much of my personal sense of femininity was wrapped up in these mammary appendages. While Ron was very reassuring and noncommittal about his preferences regarding any sort of reconstruction, my angst remained. He would always respond to my insecure probing with, "It's up to you. I'll support any decision you make."

On one level, I believed him and appreciated his openhearted support, but on the other, I secretly wondered if he was just being nice and would ultimately be disgusted by my scars. In the end, I think I was more disgusted than he was.

As the weeks passed, the zany side of me looked for an outlet, a way to relieve the tension and heaviness of anticipation. I thus discovered that humor was one of the things God had placed in my beggar's purse, and I needed it then more than ever before! I conjured up a plan. The week before my mastectomy I invited five of my closest friends to a secret party. I dubbed it a going-away party for my breast. They were each to bring a farewell poem to my departing accessory. I served large homemade cream puffs, each topped with a Hershey's kiss (picture that). We read each other's outrageous poetry and laughed until we cried. It was just the sort of girls' night out that I needed. Here's my poem:

Mastectomy

I write this little ditty
in honor of my titty
whose stay with me
was briefer than I'd planned.
I always thought 'twas pretty,
my well-matched, fair-skinned titty,
and nestled well
within Ron Brumley's hand.
I've memories warm and witty,
and so I ask no pity.
Our time, although cut short,
was simply grand!

On the other side of surgery and reconstruction, with the happy news that no chemotherapy or radiation would be necessary, I entered the process of healing and adjusting to a new body. During early recovery, it is hard to get a sense of what your new breast will look like because of swelling, discoloration and prominent scars. As my body settled in to its new normal, I found it to be a lot like a new haircut that you hate at first, but ultimately adjust to.

It took a while for me to accept the look, but within a year I rarely thought of cancer, and I actually forgot what my breast had looked like pre-surgery. The new breast, however mismatched, became fully incorporated into my psyche, and I was no longer shocked in front of a mirror. Anyway, clothing is a tremendous barrier between reality and perception.

I know that many people who survive cancer gain a new sense of purpose in life and a resolve not to waste one precious moment. I experienced no great re-evaluation of my life. In fact, my friend Roberta recently asked me, "When you head into surgery, do you wonder if you're right with God in case you die on the table?"

"No," I replied. "I think, 'I'm sure glad I don't have to be awake for this procedure!'"

I'm called to spirituality by other means. The lessons I learned were not in one magnificent epiphany, but rather in many smaller, but extremely valuable lessons about trust in God and insight into my own character. I confirmed many things I had sort of theoretically believed about God, and I got to know myself better.

The truth is I'm not afraid of being dead. It's the dying

part I dislike. I love the thought of being in heaven and finally seeing God. I try to avoid thinking of all the painful, frightening, undignified ways I might die. I hope this is in response to Jesus' command not to worry (Matthew 6:25), but it could be that I just like the comfort of denial. I don't spend much time trying to discern that fine line.

4

FAITH'S BASIS

It is helpful that faith is defined for us as "being sure of what we hope for and certain of what we do not see" (Hebrews 11:1). But it takes the rest of the Bible to give us a basis for that kind of blind trust. There are multiple, extraordinary components of that hope and certainty. Faith means completely staking my (eternal) life on a specific doctrine, laying my most troubling worries and fears at the feet of an unseen God, and walking away in peace, knowing he has heard and is in control. It means coping with life's disappointments and tragedies and remaining confident of God's love; finding reason for joy in the midst of unspeakable sorrow; learning to deal with disillusionment when people fail or betray us, without blaming God. People of faith have invested themselves in a wild commitment.

God himself is the basis for that kind of faith, and it takes a lifetime of getting to know him more and more deeply in order to feed and confirm faith. Without a growing knowledge of God, faith will die. Satan is always at work trying to erode our faith, hoping to make it crumble entirely.

Sometime in my early twenties I realized that I had never explored the Bible on my own, but had simply accepted the faith of my mother, based largely on my admiration of her sweetness and sincerity. But I found later that I didn't feel secure in the prospect of standing before God one day and saying I had lived my life based on my mother's faith. I needed to come to my own convictions based on a personal search for God.

In the period of that one year, I read through the Bible three times. The first time I filled a notebook with questions (I still have that notebook). But as I continued to read, the questions either got answered or became irrelevant as I saw the emerging nature of God. I saw his heart, his longing for an intimate relationship, and after the very first sin (Genesis 3:6), his immediate initiation of a complex and outrageously sacrificial plan that would solve our sin problems forever if we'd let him.

Even so, as I face life's struggles and disappointments, I have to call myself to depend on who God is. *His* nature is my faith's anchor. *My* nature is my obstacle. I see this most clearly when I contemplate the story of Abraham being asked to sacrifice Isaac. It is emotionally jarring to try to put myself in Abraham's shoes. And how did Isaac

go on through life without years of therapy on a psychia-
trist's couch? After all, I think I might have recurring
nightmares if my father had tied me up, laid me on an
altar and raised a knife over my heart, fully intending to
sacrifice me.

Abraham's anchor of faith was in the nature of God as
recorded in Hebrews 11:17–19:

> By faith Abraham, when God tested him, offered
> Isaac as a sacrifice. He who had received the prom-
> ises was about to sacrifice his one and only son,
> even though God had said to him, "It is through
> Isaac that your offspring will be reckoned."
> Abraham reasoned that God could raise the dead,
> and figuratively speaking, he did receive Isaac back
> from death.

It does not come naturally to me to reason the way
Abraham did. I fear that if I were in his situation, I might
have reasoned that God is undependable and capricious
at best, and a sadistic liar at worst. I would surely not
have risen early the next morning (Genesis 22:3) to make
my way to the place of sacrifice, carrying all the necessary
tools of death. I'd have probably delayed, wailing and
arguing and bitterly accusing God. I would have considered his promise broken. And I fear I would have broken
my covenant of faithfulness to him by refusing to obey his

command. Sorry to admit all this, but that is the faithless way I can sometimes reason. Without this biblical example of Abraham, I doubt I would even have a concept of a different way of reasoning to aim for.

Abraham didn't even consider that God would fail to keep his promise. He stretched his imagination to conjure a situation in which Isaac was dead, but God could still use Isaac to share in fathering the Israelite nation. He *reasoned* that God could raise Isaac from the dead. His faith in the dependable goodness and power of God remained steady. To this point, as far as biblical record conveys, God had not raised anyone from the dead, so it seems quite remarkable that Abraham even considered this solution.

I don't like to stretch my imagination to dream of possible ways God might pull a negative situation out of the muck. I want some guarantees. I want God to tell me exactly what is going to happen, and then I want him to come through—quickly! That's my nature. But Abrahamic faith is different from mine. As soon as he came up with an idea about how his omnipotent God might solve the problem of a deceased seed-bearer to fulfill the promise, he took obedient action.

God seems to have a sacrificial test for all of us. There is something in most of our lives on which we can stake our security and joy. Just as with the rich young ruler, the love of money can be the test of our faith (Matthew 19:16–22). If so, then giving generously to God is a significant obstacle. Factoring God into our budgets can frighten us and make us question his wisdom. For others, it is sacrificing career paths that would lead away from God. Other times it is clear that romantic entanglements with unbelievers must be ended (2 Corinthians 6:14). God asks some to give up recreational activities that prevent them from seeking the kingdom first (Matthew 6:33).

One sacrifice that was especially difficult for me was committing myself to God's standards for relationships. Selfish, insecure and introverted, I was frightened by the vulnerability and time commitment required for spiritual friendships. When I committed myself to obeying the Bible's standard for relationships, I felt I was diving off a high dive into ice water. I just closed my eyes and jumped. I didn't *reason* that I'd fall in love with people or that God would fill innumerable unexplored needs in my life through my friends or teach me valuable lessons, but that is what he did.

Now when I face a command of God that my nature resists, it always helps to go back to an exercise in Abraham's way of reasoning. First, I remind myself that God knows what is best for me, and I do not. My inability to see how an apparently bad situation could work for good does not reflect the limitations of God. Abraham's best scenario involved God raising Isaac from the dead, yet God's better plan was to intervene before Isaac was sacrificed. I can depend on God's ability and willingness to resolve any problem even if his solution is not exactly what I have dreamed up. He knows how to do it, and his way is always better than mine!

Next, I reconfirm my faith in God's nature: He loves me; he is faithful; his purposes are beyond my understanding; he longs for me to grow in my trust in him; he weeps when I weep, but he has never promised to take away my reasons for weeping; his power is unlimited; and he has promised to make "all things work for the good of those who love him" (Romans 8:28). That's enough! These are the truths tucked firmly in my beggar's purse that I return to again and again to ground me.

It is who I know God to be that is the basis for my faith.

5

CHARACTER AND CHANGE

Years ago, someone pointed out to me that the Ten Commandments (Exodus 20:1–17) are all about relationships: the first four about our relationship with God and the last six about our relationships with each other. This revelation about God's moral code being rooted in our regard of others was a challenge to me.

When Ron and I were first married, one of our recurring arguments went something like this:

> Ron: You are so aloof around people; you seem like a snob.
>
> Me: Well, that's just the way I am. You married me that way, and you need to get used to it.
>
> Ron: No, you need to change. You need to be more friendly.
>
> Me: Yeah? Well, you embarrass me! In a grocery store line you know everybody's life story by the time we get to check-out.
>
> Ron: Well, you'd do well to be more like that!

Personality tests peg me as an introvert. No surprise.

Being a loner is my most comfortable natural state. While I have learned to enjoy people, their personalities and ideas, I find socializing difficult. If I were to bow to my natural inclinations, I would read about people rather than interact with them. In fact, when I am in a crowd, I often feel an urgent need to escape, which I can only describe as a combination of fatigue and claustrophobia— with conversation being my confinement.

I'm a bit embarrassed to admit this for two reasons. The first is that it makes me appear antisocial, and I dislike the implications of the term. I have no disregard for others, only a proclivity for measured amounts of interaction. The second is that I fear people will tiptoe around me, trying not to offend, and I never want others to bear that burden because I really like them too much. I feel it is my responsibility to balance this innate predisposition with the selflessness and others-centeredness God encourages, rather than other people's responsibility to accommodate me.

When I confess my introversion to people, I'm often met with skepticism, which is encouraging and affirming of the changes God has worked in my character. It is not hypocrisy that makes me happy and loquacious in a crowd; it is a true joy in people—it just has some limitations that I balance with a desire to be like Jesus:

Rather, clothe yourselves with the Lord Jesus Christ, and do not think about how to gratify the desires of the sinful nature. (Romans 13:14)

Therefore, as God's chosen people, holy and dearly loved, clothe yourselves with compassion, kindness, humility, gentleness and patience. (Colossians 3:12)

All of you, clothe yourselves with humility toward one another.... (1 Peter 5:5)

The predominate idea of clothing something is to cover up something else. But I resist this idea. The Christian life couldn't be much fun if it just consists of trying to hide something behind a pretty façade. I love the nature of God in every aspect, and I want it to permeate me, not just clothe me. But the clothing bit is my part and the permeating bit is God's part.

During Jesus' last days on earth, he intensified his efforts to help his disciples understand their mission after his death. They were understandably confused and distressed. He reassured them: "Do not let your hearts be troubled. Trust in God; trust also in me" (John 14:1).

He went on to help them understand what their future would be like without him, emphasizing the great gift and mystery of the indwelling of the Holy Spirit:

> "If you love me, you will obey what I command. And I will ask the Father, and he will give you another Counselor to be with you forever—the Spirit of truth. The world cannot accept him, because it neither sees him nor knows him. But you know him, for he lives with you and will be in you.... I am in my Father, and you are in me, and I am in you....
>
> "If anyone loves me, he will obey my teaching. My Father will love him, and we will come to him and make our home with him." (John 14:15–17, 20, 23)

Throughout the Bible, God makes an inseparable connection between love and obedience. It is loving him and loving his character that makes it a joy and not a burden to obey. It is love that enables perseverance and keeps us from growing weary and burning out.

I've heard people say (and have probably said myself) that it would have been easier to believe, easier to be zealous, easier to obey if we had the advantage of walking with Jesus, seeing his miracles, hearing his teaching and being personally coached by him to live godly lives. Surprisingly, Jesus here contradicts that supposition:

> "But I tell you the truth: It is for your good that I am going away. Unless I go away, the Counselor will not come to you; but if I go, I will send him to you." (John 16:7)

Astonishing! He's saying that it is better for them (and,

by implication, for us) for Jesus to be *in* them than to be *with* them! Jesus within—how amazing is that! While we may not in this lifetime understand all that it means to have the Spirit of God within us, we find a few fascinating hints in the New Testament.

For one thing, even with his powerful presence within us, we do not have to obey his urgings. We can suppress the righteous inclinations he stirs in us. That must be why Paul told the Thessalonians not to "put out the Spirit's fire" (1 Thessalonians 5:19). It must be that when we choose to do other than the will of God that we "grieve the Holy Spirit of God" (Ephesians 4:30). There he is, working so hard within us to persuade us to do right, and when we choose not to, he reacts emotionally with grief.

While it is true that through love and obedience we have to do our part, the role God plays is an ocean compared to our tiny droplet:

> Therefore, my dear friends, as you have always obeyed—not only in my presence, but now much more in my absence—continue to work out your salvation with fear and trembling, for it is God who works in you to will and to act according to his good purpose. (Philippians 2:12–13)

It is wonderfully encouraging to know that God is tenacious in his efforts to help us grow in our righteousness.

Earlier in Paul's letter to the Philippians, he reassured them:

> "...he who began a good work in you will carry it on
> to completion until the day of Christ Jesus."
> (Philippians 1:6)

Also consider these passages that show God's involvement in our character changes:

> May God himself, the God of peace, sanctify you
> through and through. May your whole spirit, soul and
> body be kept blameless at the coming of our Lord
> Jesus Christ. The one who calls you is faithful and he
> will do it. (1 Thessalonians 5:23–24)

> ...By one sacrifice he has made perfect forever
> those who are being made holy. (Hebrews 10:14)

As we work to obey God and clothe ourselves with the nature of Christ, God is at work within us, shaping our characters to increasingly reflect his own. Through his Spirit he nudges us to think and behave in ways that fulfill his divine purposes for our lives—to fulfill our destinies. Even the most stubborn parts of our sinful natures will eventually yield to the Spirit of God if we persevere.

I can't help but think how I would never have come to this understanding on my own. It is only God's word, his Holy Spirit, his faithful answers to prayer that change us to be increasingly like him. These are the treasures in my beggar's purse straight from his hand, supplying transforming grace.

These days you are likely to find me glancing into the shopping cart behind me in line and commenting to the shopper, "I almost bought that fish, but I'm afraid to cook it. How do you prepare it?" Or, "I love your bag! Can we be best friends so I can come over and borrow it sometime?" I'm still not as good at this as Ron is, but I feel a sense of victory every time I start a happy conversation with a stranger. I always look for an opportunity in those encounters to bring up God. At last, it's fun for me.

6

PRAYER

There are mysteries about prayer and God's responses that we may not understand until heaven. We don't know how God decides on responses to our prayers. When I was a little girl, I remember asking my mother, "If I pray to God that it won't rain and someone else is praying that it *will* rain, how does God decide which prayer to answer?" I don't remember Mom trying to answer that one.

In Matthew 7:7, Jesus said, "Ask and it will be given to you; seek and you will find; knock and the door will be opened to you." What is the difference between asking, seeking and knocking? Let's look at some things we know about God that can help us understand this three-pronged approach to prayer.

Ask

We are dependent on God and need to come to him with our requests. Even Jesus, while he was on earth and confined by human limitations, was dependent on God in prayer. In Matthew 6:11, Jesus prayed, "Give us today our daily bread." This is sort of amazing since Jesus, the ultimate miracle-worker, could have snapped his fingers and created a feast. God likes for us to come to him and talk to him and express our need for him. He blesses us all the time, but he apparently doesn't want us to assume that because he is all-knowing and benevolent, he is going to read our minds and grant our every wish, even if our wishes are virtuous. It is not his plan to fulfill our every wish, and certainly not without a relationship and a conversation.

When I was eight or nine years old, my friend Mary Ellen and I faced an irreconcilable difference about what we wanted to play together. I considered myself a Christian and Mary Ellen a reprobate, so somewhere into our heated argument, I said, "Let's pray." We sat on the little rug in her bedroom, and I led us in a prayer asking God to help us be friendly and to play happily together. When I got home I related this story to my mother who asked, "And did God answer your prayer?"

"No," I said, "but I didn't want Mary Ellen to know that, so I just played what she wanted to."

"I think God answered your prayer," my mother replied.

I think so, too. I think he always does, but I think we can be too obtuse to see the answers and too negligent to voice our requests. So often, prayer is an afterthought. I'm ashamed to admit this is true in my life, even though I've had zillions of reminders over the years that prayer should be my first line of defense. It usually is if I'm facing a crisis, but it's the everydayness of my needs that seems to keep me from recognizing my dependence.

As I mentioned, Jesus prayed, "Give us today our daily bread." It's rare that I pray this since my pantry is full, but if I were starving, I'd be prostrate, begging for sustenance. In many areas I neglect a fully humble dependence on God, as if I've got it covered without his help. On the other hand, in my defense, if I were to try to pray about every individual thing that sustains my life, I'd be on my knees around the clock and never get anything else done. But since I'm so far from that extreme, there is a healthy amount of conviction I need to embrace. When I'm really on point with this issue, prayer is an ongoing conversation throughout my day with a friend whose presence I'm continually aware of.

Seek

I'm not sure I'm right about my view on this aspect of prayer, but I've found that I need to pray more expectantly and be looking for (seeking) the answers (Psalm 5:1–3). They don't always come in the package I expect them to come in. A stunning example of this is a prayer I prayed years ago about our small congregation in San Diego. I felt we were so anonymous, and that seemed very wrong. There was nothing under the radar about the ministry of Jesus. I wanted our church to be making enough impact to be noticed. I began praying that God would shine a spotlight on our faith and good deeds so we could be increasingly effective in our community.

Shortly afterwards, a young woman became a Christian in our church. Her mother was an atheist and was very opposed to her daughter's newfound faith. The mother wrote a guest editorial for our local newspaper and then began picketing our church services. The next thing we knew, our little body of believers was on the front page of the paper with pictures of our faithful picketer out front.

I was asking for admiration not infamy. I don't think God misheard my request; I just think he had a better plan. But he for sure answered my prayers. Our little church was no longer anonymous!

"Ask and it will be given to you" may mean "Ask and an answer will be given to you." The answer may be "no," but it will be a powerful answer with God's eternal purposes in mind. Therefore, we may have to seek to find what that answer is lest we keep looking for the wrong thing.

Knock

I think this may have to do with persistence. No one ever gives one tap to a door they hope to have opened. We give all kind of rhythmic raps and then repeat, sometimes multiple times, before we give up. The more hopeful we are that someone is home and will respond, the louder and longer we knock.

Persistence is an aspect of prayer that God advocates. I don't know why. My mother used to get really upset with me if I continued pleading for something after a first request. Sometimes it was the annoyance of my persistence that provoked her frustrated denial of my request. Wrapping my head around God's love of persistence took some spiritual gymnastics. But Jesus illustrated God's desire for persistent prayer in his parable of the widow in Luke 18:1–8: "…yet because this widow keeps bothering me, I will see that she gets justice…."

Isn't that amazing? God wants us to *bother* him. I love that. I know I give up too soon and sometimes even think I am surrendering to the will of God. Apparently God has a different view of what I consider to be nagging!

Who knows what other elements of prayer fall under the category of knocking? Perhaps fasting or requesting the intercessory prayer of others or spending the entire night in prayer. There is evidence in the Bible that our prayers get a different kind of attention from God if we fast or have others join in our petitions. But whatever choices we make in approaching God, we should go with humble hearts, spreading our beggar's purses before him and expecting treasures to be added to our cloths. He is faithful. We may not immediately recognize the value of his offerings in our purses, but we can be guaranteed it is just what we need.

This is a great formula for our prayer lives. Tell God what you want. Look for his answer. It may not come in the way you expect it, so you may have to do some spiritual detective work. Bother God with repetition. Let him know you mean it. Let him see you put some effort into expressing your desires instead of expecting all the effort to flow from him as he answers.

7

LEARNING OBEDIENCE

During childhood I idolized my mother. I think this is normal for most children. Even when I reached an age at which I could detect her imperfections, I still found her positive qualities—mostly her unconditional love for me—to overwhelmingly outweigh the negative. I've always had great clarity about the things that I loved about her.

She was unfailingly patient. She had a wonderful laugh, and it rang out daily. She encouraged me through every failure. In fact, she would never acknowledge that I failed. She could put a positive spin on any disaster. She had a loyal and supportive little band of best friends who shared one another's joys and sorrows.

A hard worker, she put in punishingly long hours running my dad's business. She was my on-call tutor for homework and my last-minute project completer. She had many creative talents, but her own pursuits were put on the back burner in order to meet the needs of others. She was a tireless servant, caring for my long-ill father and then her mother and aunt until their deaths.

Loving and admiring her engaged my whole heart in wanting to obey the Bible's command to "honor your father and mother" (Ephesians 6:2 and Exodus 20:12). I deemed her exceedingly worthy of my honor.

As a widow she moved in with Ron and me in 1986. We were delighted for the opportunity to serve her and longed to make her life a joy in every way that we could. She moved from house to house and state to state with us seven times as different ministry assignments demanded our relocation. She was a trooper about these late-life disruptions to her routines and relationships.

In 2002, she was diagnosed with Alzheimer's disease. One of the unfortunate lessons she had taught me about dealing with problems was to remain in denial for as long as possible. We both indulged in this luxurious folly regarding her progressive loss of memory until it reached a crisis level. Then it came time for me to play catch-up, trying to learn how to cope with the ravages of her anxiety and confusion, because she could no longer participate with me in those adjustments. I did not yet find the wisdom I needed for this situation in my beggar's purse.

I was slow to catch on. I wanted her back. It felt as if I was losing her a piece at a time. I kept trying to reorient her, which is the very thing one shouldn't do. The mantra for the Alzheimer's caregiver has to be "go with them into their world; they cannot come back into yours." It was agonizing.

She walked into our living room one day, where we had the same furniture and decor that she had lived with for the past fourteen years. She stood gazing at the old family photos that were hung on the wall and said tentatively, "Oh, this is Aunt Bertha and Uncle Charlie's house, isn't it? I've always loved it here." My insensitive response was "No! This is our house. You live with us. You've lived with us for years. This is the living room." I took her by the hand and led her down the hall. "This is your bedroom. Look. These are all your things."

After my mom's death, I was relaying a similar incident to my daughter Gretchen and weeping over my regret and failure to become more quickly what my mother needed. Gretchen wisely and gently asked, "What do you wish you had done instead?"

I wish I had said: "Do you like it here? Let's sit down and reminisce about Aunt Bertha and Uncle Charlie. How does it feel to be in their home?" I wish I had hugged her instead of pulling her down the hall. I wish I had made her feel safe and welcome in the strange new world she was entering instead of futilely trying to force her to rejoin me in mine. I was in anguish, trying to hang on to something that was inevitably slipping away.

Most painful was her no longer recognizing me. Every hour with each interaction, the loss of her memory of me made me feel a loss of the place I had once held in her heart. She alternately called me Loreen or Dottie, her cousin and sister respectively, her childhood playmates. But I wanted to be Linda again, with the intimacy of the bond between a mother and daughter.

One day she was telling (and retelling and retelling) an anecdote about one of her rancher father's cowhands named Fritz. We were in the car, and I was surprised to find my fingers tightening on the steering wheel in rage. I felt a spontaneous fury rise within me that quickly hardened into a bitter resentment toward Fritz. I hated him for having a protected lodging in my mother's memory when I had none. Within minutes the hatred dissolved into tragic amusement as I realized the folly of blaming poor Fritz for Mom's regression.

Against my will I was daily escorted to an open grave, which was filling fragment by fragment with the tattered remains of one of my most treasured relationships. I was slow to relinquish my need for the bond and to allow that need to be filled by God. This kept me from effectively meeting my mom's emotional needs. As my friend Shanti told me: "As long as you are so upset, you are making your mom's illness about you instead of letting it be about her."

I joined support groups and subscribed to the Alzheimer's Association newsletter. I tapped my resources, calling friends whose parents had suffered from this disease. I got great advice, but some of it didn't make sense to me until it was too late. I tried to wrap my head around what was happening and what the future held.

There is a double-edged sword awaiting the loved ones of Alzheimer's patients. One side prods you to happily accept becoming a stranger to your loved one. The other side forces you to adjust to them becoming a stranger to you. In my own case, my mother, whose life-long persona exuded sweetness and gentleness, became sometimes irritable, argumentative and stubborn. She hated being bathed, and on one occasion, tightened her little hand into a fist and socked me in the face in a shocking demonstration of protest.

I panicked when she turned on all her stove burners and oven to heat the kitchen, when she wandered off to "go home," when she lost her purse and lost it again, and when she let strangers, salesmen, into her little apartment within our house. Several times a day she packed to "go home" insisting that she was only visiting and her stay had lasted too long. In frustration, I unpacked her things and tried to persuade her to lengthen her stay. I struggled to keep her medications straight, balance her checkbook and document her eligibility for Medicaid. I soothed her hysteria when she couldn't find her mother. I tried to be at peace entering her reality, which should have been a simple act of pretending, but for me it was a participation in a horribly painful fantasy. Every instinctive inclination within me screamed out to make her remember who we were to one another.

It felt like I was lying to my mother. For me these were bizarre fabrications, like "Tuck [my deceased father] called to say he's okay, but stuck in traffic, and he'll be home late" (this in response to her anxiety that Dad was not there). I was not fearful that she'd be upset when he failed to arrive because by the time she would ordinarily be alarmed again, she'd have forgotten her original concern. Most painful of all for me was pretending to be whoever she thought I was in the moment and cheerfully interacting with her, playing the role of someone else. I didn't learn these things soon enough to keep me from adding months to her pain and confusion.

I found it very hard to forgive myself after the crisis passed and objective thinking returned. In my prayers I apologized again and again to God, asking his forgiveness for my failure to honor my mother through her final trial. I struggled as much or more than I ever had to get my feet on solid ground emotionally. Grief, fear, frustration and confusion were my companions, as well as hers. Unfortunately, it is not the purity or intensity of our vision that accomplishes our noblest aspirations. Our own imperfect natures become the barricades against our best intentions. In other words, having a desire to do what is best doesn't always enable us to do it.

I didn't turn the corner on consistently becoming what she needed me to be until she was in a nursing home and the twenty-four hour pressure was relieved. I certainly experienced all the guilt and uncertainty many speak of when deciding to place their loved one in a care facility, but for me and for Mom, it was the right decision. I learned to enjoy her again, even though so little was left of the mom I had known for so long. Love was able to dominate my interactions with her again; not fear and frustration and fatigue.

Still, the time I had with her to "do it right" did not absolve the guilt I felt for the occasions I had done it wrong. More than anything, I wished to have been a constant blessing to her. Reassurances from my friends who had walked through that terrible time with me did little to absolve my angst. My reference point for extending grace to myself and beginning to heal came from these scriptures about Jesus' life on earth:

> For we do not have a high priest who is unable to

sympathize with our weaknesses, but we have one who has been tempted in every way, just as we are—yet was without sin. (Hebrews 4:15)

Although he was a son, he learned obedience from what he suffered and, once made perfect, he became the source of eternal salvation for all who obey him. (Hebrews 5:8–9)

Alzheimer's was an unfamiliar path for me. I had never walked that way before nor been a close witness to anyone else who had. Jesus came to earth, and every path he walked here was new to him, yet he never sinned. I, on the other hand, grope along and stumble and hurt myself and others around me. I am desperately in need of forgiveness and salvation! And that's the point. That's why he came: because I'm hopeless without him. When he learned obedience, he did it perfectly. I'm down here learning obedience, and perfection is my aim (2 Corinthians 13:11), but I've never done anything perfectly. I'm happy with the times I've come closest, but the gap between my best efforts and perfection is pretty wide, and only the blood of Jesus makes up the difference.

If I walk that path of caregiver again, which I desperately hope I never do, I think I might come closer to obedience (for me, in this context, that would mean consistently displaying the fruit of the Spirit in Galatians 5:22–23). I'll find out then whether I really learned anything from my experience with Mom—whether I stored helpful spiritual lessons in my beggar's purse.

I think, I hope, that now I'd be calmer, love better, adapt sooner, laugh more and make decisions with greater sureness. In the meantime, I pray the lessons I learned can benefit and comfort others who are trying to get their bearings on that dark and rocky path.

8

VALUABLE IN GOD'S SIGHT

Some time ago, a friend of mine was telling me about her unfaithfulness to her husband, her efforts to repent and her interactions with a Christian counselor. The counselor had explained to her that since her early teens, she had most likely tried to find her worth in being attractive to men and that she needed to understand how valuable she was to God.

I see the counselor's point. Our value to God is amazing, thrilling and compelling. But it is also illogical. Our value to God is not because of our inherent worth. Indeed, our value to God says more about God than it says about us. It's important to separate these issues: We are immeasurably valuable to God, while being inherently without any value at all (Romans 3:9–18). This paradox teaches us that he is merciful and compassionate. It teaches us that it is God's nature to love us unconditionally, to long for relationship with us, to be eager to forgive us, and to be willing to shape us into blessings to the world around us.

Even our good deeds are unfit. Isaiah says they are filthy rags (Isaiah 64:6). That's a bitter pill to swallow! The best I can do is not enough, so why try at all? In truth, if we can get our eyes off ourselves long enough to fall in love with God, it all makes sense. The love of Christ compels us to change (2 Corinthians 5:14), not a self-improvement program that helps us like ourselves better. God wants our good deeds to be a response to his love, not an effort to love ourselves or make someone else love us. He *already* loves us beyond our wildest dreams!

We are the apple of his eye (Psalm 17:8). Don't we all long to be adored like that? Well, that is how God feels about us. We light up his eyes with delight. We are each individually his happy obsession. We have his complete attention 24/7 (Psalm 139:2–5). There is no threat to his fidelity to us. No fickleness threatens his desire for us to belong to him. God's love is the magnificent love we all innately need and long for.

Like many young women I know, I was once in angst over my need to feel loved, appreciated and valued. It affected every aspect of my life. On the spiritual side, I valued goodness, so I tried to do enough good deeds and talk spiritually enough to psych myself into believing I had moral value and something to offer God. On the worldly side, I aimed for a sense of worth through my appearance, wit, possessions and social acceptance. Such a pursuit was tiring and frustrating.

The back story to all this may be rooted in my relationship with my father as I perceived it. My dad was a good guy. I fully believe he loved me with all his heart, but had no idea how to show that to an adolescent girl. From my perspective, he only spoke to me when he needed to correct me. In the meantime I was dancing as fast as I could to get his attention and approval.

I remember bringing home straight A's in high school and longing for him to verbalize his pride in me. I even eavesdropped on his conversations for a couple of days hoping he would brag on me to someone. No luck. When I modeled a new dress for him, I longed to be told I was pretty. Instead, as I remember, he reserved his comments for an assessment of whether my apparel was sufficiently modest. If it failed his modesty test, I was sent back to the store to return it. I know this was evidence of his love, but that was hard for a teenage girl to discern. There are no perfect parents, so most of us are going to have to find our security in God.

The tricky little nuance in seeing our value to God is in understanding that our worth emanates from the heart of God, not from our behavior. We need to just relax and admit that we are unworthy of redemption and then glory in the redemption of God. I only have value in the hands of God. He can use me and do great things. The best things I have ever done reflect the glory of God, not the glory of me. I don't even get credit for the impulse to do a good deed. The apostle Paul disabused me of that notion when he wrote, "It is God who works in you to will and to act according to his good purpose" (Philippians 2:13).

I see so many women struggle and struggle to feel a sense of worth. It creates a kind of self-centeredness and insecurity that is counterproductive to their goal of being at peace with who they are. We can never find happiness by looking inward. But we can find pure joy by looking at who God is and how he feels about us. It is about falling in love with God.

The sustaining aspect of this kind of motivating, fulfilling love comes from our lifelong efforts to know him in deeper and deeper ways. I think it's amusing the way Paul tried to explain this to the Ephesians with an apparent contradiction, saying he prayed for them to know the love of God which surpasses knowledge. Know the unknowable (Ephesians 3:19). Ponder that for a while.

This seeming conundrum brings a richer meaning to seeking God. It's a search that has no end. You don't ever come to a point in life where you can say, "Got it. Found

God. Mission accomplished!" If we live to be 100 and have spent every day searching for new insights into the nature of God, we will come to the last day of our lives having only skimmed the surface of all that he is—his holiness, his omniscience, his righteousness, his purity, his humility, his perfection, his purposes; there is no end. We are finite and have little capacity for the infinite, but are magnificently blessed by whatever little glimpses of God we can embrace and treasure.

Getting caught up in knowing God is the true source of freedom from getting caught up in ourselves and agonizing over trying to like ourselves. It is hard being human, and earth is a hard place to live. But even without having God as a reference point, the unspiritual world wisely, if harshly, admonishes: "Get over yourself!" That's a tough assignment unless you learn to bask in the adoration of God. And this can only come from getting to know him.

9

Resembling Daddy

When children are small, it's adorable to watch them try to be grown-up by imitating their parents. I love seeing a little boy try to saunter, hands in pockets like his dad, or a little girl sit in front of a mirror experimenting with her mother's makeup.

When my daughter Meredith was a teen, people would mistake her voice for mine when she answered the phone. Hearing someone exclaim: "Meredith sounds so much like you; I thought it was you when she answered the phone!" brought a special joy to my heart. I pondered this response. Was it pride? Yes, in a way, but not the kind of pride in which I could take credit for something.

After all, I had spent no effort training her to sound like me, and sounding like me was no special virtue. And she was not practicing vocal mimicry in order to affect my tone. Yet, I could actually feel the swelling in my chest with the satisfaction I felt, knowing she sounded like me. It marked her as uniquely mine. I could give dozens of other illustrations that gave me similar satisfaction with each of my children.

I finally concluded that my joy came from the evidence of connection, a stamp of belonging. It sort of advertised that she was mine, and my delight in her made me want everyone to know she was my daughter! It's how parents feel when they hear the comparisons: "He has his dad's wit," or "She has her mother's eyes."

That is how God feels about us, yet our resemblance to our heavenly Father will be a matter of intention, not of genetic happenstance. And it will be a matter of heart and character, not appearance or mannerisms. Paul explains this in Ephesians 5:1–2:

> Be imitators of God, therefore, as dearly loved children and live a life of love, just as Christ loved us and gave himself up for us as a fragrant offering and sacrifice to God.

We are God's "dearly loved children" and he wants us to look like him in our character. He wants us to see the world through his eyes and extend the kind of love he has for all his creation. That will surely not come naturally to mere mortals. Because we need a living example to even know what that looks like, God came to earth in the form of his Son and lived out a love we could imitate.

The tricky thing about imitation is that it feels fake— and it is. Satan loves to accuse us of being phony when we're trying to adopt into our character the perfect qualities of God. He loves to create an inner turmoil with accusations of hypocrisy when we are just trying to be adoring children. But God loves it when we're making the effort to take on his nature. He doesn't consider it phony at all. On the contrary, he knows that it is hard for us to work against our own natures to try to be like him. In fact, it's what we were born for; it's our destiny!

The apostle Peter addresses this process in 2 Peter 1. He explains that we are honored by God with the invitation to "participate in the divine nature." Wow! We can share in the very nature and Spirit of God, himself (v4). This is an amazing possibility! How will this occur? Will we wake up one day and miraculously respond to every life circumstance the way God would—the way he *did* when he was here on earth? No, Peter explains the process—it's about imitation and *it isn't easy*! He says,

> Make every effort to add to your faith goodness; and to goodness, knowledge; and to knowledge, self-control; and to self-control, perseverance; and to perseverance, godliness; and to godliness, brotherly kindness; and to brotherly kindness, love. (2 Peter 1:5–7)

It can feel a little overwhelming. It's a lot of work. None of these things come naturally for me and, at best, they are developed over time with much focus and effort.

This is a little discouraging on the one hand, since I admire these qualities and aspire to them, but I wish they were easier to internalize. I wish I could just pray to be more like God and wake up the next morning alarmingly holy! While the Spirit certainly aids us in every godly endeavor, he doesn't eliminate our role in striving to put on the nature of God.

On the other hand, it's encouraging to know my Father believes in me and is cheering me on in my efforts. I won't resemble God in his bone structure or his facial features, but I can grow to look more like him in my character. I hope he's looking down from heaven feeling the same sweet connection and affectionate possessiveness I enjoy with my own children. I hope he's turning to some angel and remarking: "She's looking more like me every day!"

10

A QUIET SPIRIT

This quality of character that God values in women—a gentle and quiet spirit—does not usually come naturally (1 Peter 3:4). It certainly does not come naturally for me. I aspire to a gentle and quiet spirit, yet in a crunch, my nature is more prone to anxiety, rashness and hysteria.

It seems I must have passed these traits along to my oldest daughter (sorry, Meredith). But she's a wise and spiritual woman who reaches out for the lessons God has for her in trials, so she's been able to bless me with things she learns, sharing insights from her beggar's purse to add to mine. A few years ago, during an emotionally chaotic period in her life, we were talking on the phone daily. She was grasping for any spiritual anchor to stabilize her and offer her inner peace, direction and hope. She could not sense God's presence and intervention, and it sent her into a panic. I wanted desperately to be a comfort to her, but ultimately it was her own discovery from within her beggar's purse that brought comfort to us both. In constant prayer, she stayed alert to any instruction God would give her.

She called me one day to say, "Mom, you know how mothers always tell their children: 'If we're in a crowd and we get separated, just stand still, and I will find you'? I realized that is what God is saying to me. I'm frantically spinning around trying to find God's hand to cling to, and it's my very rushing that is keeping me from him. I just need to be still, and he will find me."

Easier said than done, and yet this is what God tells us to do. I think we long for God to solve all our problems. He doesn't promise to fix every circumstance of our lives so that we can find peace. He wants our peace to come from our trust in him, even while the storms are still raging. Remember how Moses reassured a panicked Israel: "The LORD will fight for you; you need only to be still" (Exodus 14:14). God was expecting them to calm down even before they knew how he would resolve the problem of the pursuit of Pharaoh's army. He'd given them some evidence of his faithfulness to warrant this kind of trust—the ten plagues had just rendered their enemy practically impotent. Still, the urgency of the immediate danger loomed large.

In similar circumstances, God recommends the same quietness for us.

> "Be still and know that I am God." (Psalm 46:10)

> "Be still before the Lord, all mankind, because he has roused himself from his holy dwelling." (Zechariah 2:13)

David must have understood that he had a role to play in quieting down because he says in Psalm 131:2–3:

> But I have stilled and quieted my soul;
>> like a weaned child with its mother,
>> like a weaned child is my soul within me.
> O, Israel, put your hope in the LORD
>> both now and forevermore.

We get a clue here about how to quiet our souls. It has to do with putting our hope in God. His power and his love are ample evidence that he is worthy of such hope. Still, God is fully willing to help in the process, and he doesn't just sit back waiting for us to pull it together, although it may not be on our time schedule. Consider the combined message of the following passages:

> The LORD your God is with you,
>> He is mighty to save.
> He will take great delight in you,
>> He will quiet you with his love,
>> He will rejoice over you with singing.
> (Zephaniah 3:7)

Be still before the LORD and wait patiently for him.
(Psalm 37:7)

Recently, I was waiting for cancer surgery to be scheduled. Every time the phone rang, I hoped I would finally get word of a date so I would know how to plan accordingly. (Many cancer patients admit that since their cancer is so outside their control, they long to feel in control of everything else that they can—including their schedules.)

My friend Angela Johnson understood my need to be still, and my temptation not to be, and she reached out to encourage me with this poem she had written:

I stand as still as I can to let the world whirl about
me.
The leaves outside my window submit to the slightest nudge from the wind,
And no harm befalls them.
It is as if the leaves know more than I.
They understand their place, their purpose.
One tiny leaf equals the sum of the whole,
And all goes well.
Adorned with beauty, grace, a full life—
This tiny leaf.
And life it gives—
This charming leaf.
Then I move once again, at will.

I want every life circumstance to be overwhelmed by the love of God and the hope I have in him. I want to be as surrendered to his will as any inert part of his creation. I have a ways to go, but I know what I'm aiming for, and I know the lessons I can reclaim from my beggar's purse.

11

INVISIBLE BLESSINGS

On an overcast Friday afternoon, Ron and I left the apartment of friends in downtown Chicago. We had stopped by to pick up a bridal shower gift that a few gals had pitched in to buy, and we were walking to our car a couple of blocks away (the closest space we could find). The package was large and festively wrapped. We were just a few car lengths from our own vehicle, and the street was deserted, but from behind us we heard a voice.

"Hey, ya got a dollar to spare?"

We both turned to see a scruffy looking young man approaching us. Ron reached for his wallet and simultaneously said to me: "Get in the car." You'd have to know Ron to recognize the implications of the tone he used, but my kids and I knew it well. That tone meant: "Do it now; don't argue; we'll talk about it later." I obeyed.

From the front seat with the windows down, I watched Ron offer the man a couple of bills from his wallet. I noticed that the man had a light jacket slung across his right forearm, covering both his arm and his hand. He told Ron that he had a gun in that hand and wanted Ron's wallet. Ron attempted to reason with his intimidator and pleaded with him to just take his money and leave his identification and pictures of his family. No success with this suggestion—the man drew closer, waving his hand with the alleged gun and telling Ron in no uncertain terms that his demand was not negotiable. Ron handed over his wallet with its forty dollars in cash, a couple of credit cards we would have to cancel, and his Illinois driver's license that we'd have to stand in line to renew.

Both of us were completely rattled. After filing a police report (they admonished us *never* to pull out your wallet when someone asks you for money on the street), we headed for home. Our anxiety was palpable in our little Toyota as we traveled toward the western suburbs, and Ron said, "Say a prayer for us." We definitely needed the calming of the Lord.

I began my prayer trying to put into perspective the angst we were experiencing by thanking God that we were safe and that the greatest consequence of this disturbing event was $40 and a little inconvenience. We were unharmed.

This led me to begin thanking God for times he had protected us when we didn't even know we'd been in danger. No telling how many potentially hazardous occasions had occurred when God had intervened or sent his angels to shield or guide us. We had most likely gone on our way oblivious to the debt of gratitude we owed God. I was feeling humbled and grateful when a startling fact hit me.

"Ron," I interrupted my prayer and turned wide-eyed in my seat, "I was carrying a gift worth far more than the amount in your wallet. And guess what? You asked me to cash two checks today. I have $800 in my purse [an event so rare I'd probably never before had that much cash on me], but you sent me to the car, causing our mugger to ignore me while he focused on your wallet."

I didn't even remember the unusual circumstance of the sum of cash I was carrying during this ordeal. I was nervous, but I'd have probably had a breakdown if I'd thought about how much money I had. We were a little awestruck as we realized how much more we had to be thankful for than we originally realized. I think that's true every minute of our lives. How many times has God guided us away from danger, and we didn't know or were griping about some minor inconvenience instead of rejoicing in our safety?

Because we are so affected by the natural world, experiencing it with all of our senses, the unseen world is illusive unless we make a conscious effort to believe that spiritual forces exist to guide and protect us every day of our lives. The Bible is full of affirmation that God has armies of angels and other powers focused on our well-being.

I love that Deborah, in her song thanking God for the amazing victory he gave to Israel over the Canaanites, credited the stars with a role in that battle:

"From heaven the stars fought,
   from their courses they fought against Sisera."
(Judges 5:20)

I don't know what that's all about, but I hope I get a widescreen replay of that event in heaven. I want to see what God did with those stars! The flooding of the Kishon River makes sense to me: Chariot wheels get stuck in mud. But I love that Deborah "saw" how God deployed the stars and understood that the victory was entirely due to God. She still thanked the men who came out to fight and called out the cowards, but she sang a chapter-long song to thank God for his intervention that day. I think we have to slow down and use our God-given spiritual eyes to constantly believe in his presence and his working in our lives minute by minute. There are facts that we can only know by faith, but they are facts nonetheless.

The apostle Paul speaks with a confident tone while in prison at the end of his life in 2 Timothy 1:12. During a time when everything available to his five senses affirmed distress and imminent death, he relaxed and delighted in the sure knowledge that God was in control:

> I *know* whom I have believed, and am *convinced* that he is able to guard what I have entrusted to him for that day. (emphasis added)

Nothing about Paul's immediate trial affected his confidence in the unseen care and control of a trustworthy God. This is the kind of bold faith we need to invest in our daily prayers—that once we've entrusted something to God, he's got it firmly in his grip and we can anticipate his divine guarding of our lives.

12

Accepting Help

Those of us who are inclined to take care of others often have trouble being on the receiving end of assistance. This makes it hard for a community of believers to effectively obey Galatians 6:2: "Carry each other's burdens, and in this way you will fulfill the law of Christ." While givers and takers don't fall into two crisply defined categories—because most of us can gracefully be on the supplying or the receiving end of service—some of us fall at the extremes of this spectrum.

I find it hard to assess whether I really need help or not. I argue with myself: "Will I really be unable to cook for a while after that surgery? We can just eat frozen dinners." "Can't my house wait one more week to be cleaned instead of inconveniencing someone else?"

After being diagnosed with non-Hodgkin's lymphoma in 2006 and undergoing several months of chemotherapy, I was at a church staff retreat where a few women told me they felt I had not made my needs known while I was in treatment.

I don't want to be independent, and I want to be humble enough to admit I am needy, but I can't always figure it out. What I've learned about myself is that when I'm going through a difficult time, I may not have any pressing practical needs, but I have very real emotional needs. I need reassurance that I am not going through the trial alone, and that others are attentive in prayer and sympathy, and have a willingness to come to my aid—emphasis on the willingness part. Emotionally, I care more about the willing than the doing.

Years ago when my younger son was nine or ten years old, he came down with a rare intestinal disorder and was in our local hospital. Ron was out of town, so I was alone to manage the three other kids and hospital runs. His doctors decided his condition was too serious for that facility, so they sent me home to pack a bag and return to follow Matt's ambulance to our regional children's hospital. I drove home frightened and praying, and I opened my front door to find two sisters busily cleaning my house. I dissolved into tears of gratitude and found myself amazingly comforted by their hugs and encouragement.

In my bedroom changing clothes, and still crying conflicted tears of stress and joy, I realized how funny it was that I was so grateful to have my house being cleaned. The truth was, in that moment, my concern for my son trumped every other concern, and I frankly would not have cared if the house burned down if it meant Matt would be well. How much less did I care if it was clean!

But the point was not the cleanliness of the house. The point was the evidence of those sisters' care and sympathy. It washed over me like a healing balm. I've tried to remember that when I see other people in stressful situations. It doesn't matter as much what you do as that you do something, anything, to show that you care. It's nice if it meets a *real* need, but it is almost guaranteed to meet an emotional need. It fits perfectly with 1 John 3:18: "Dear children, let us not love with words or tongue, but with actions and in truth." Loving words are good, too, but there's nothing like demonstrated love!

This kind of love is hard to ask for if you are the needy one. "I need to see that you care." "I need you to want to do something to ease my pain." "I need you to demonstrate your love by sacrificing for me even if it has no practical value." Sometimes we'll say those things to a spouse, but rarely to one another.

In May 2009, I was diagnosed with breast cancer and told I would need a mastectomy (my second, since I'd already lost my left breast to cancer in 1997). I'd really prefer to deal with only one form of cancer at a time, and since non-Hodgkin's lymphoma is considered incurable (but treatable), I felt sort of maxed out on the cancer thing.

On the way home from the surgeon's office, I was dreading yet another surgery. I was also pondering those previous admonitions to let someone know my needs.

Discouragement and dread forced my hand, and I knew I had to ask for help. I was very out of sorts. But since my coping mechanisms include large doses of humor, I marched in from my visit to the surgeon and penned the following tongue-in-cheek poem of "repentance" without even pausing to take off my coat. It was a nice outlet.

Mastectomy 2009

I'm sick of being courageous!
You can keep your stiff upper lip.
I have utterly no intention
Of trying to get a grip!
I'm giving full vent to self-pity—
I'll accept any you have to spare.
I'll take all your service and fawning—
Do my nails, rub my back, fix my hair.
Come alone or in pairs or a cadre
Like a crew of industrious elves.
Be meticulous, please, while I'm taking my ease.
Dust behind all the books on my shelves.
Clean my kitchen until it sparkles.

Bring me gourmet meals every night.
Run my errands and do all my laundry—
I prefer linens crisp and white.
Send me cards until my mailman
Is bent beneath his load,
But send me no heavy reading—
My mind's in recovery mode.
Fluff my pillows and play me some music,
And then scrub my tarnished floors.
Fill my rooms with the scent of lavender,
Don't forget—dust the tops of my doors.
Get-well cards: I like them witty;
Written sentiments: sugary sweet.
Keep up this obsequious doting
Until I'm back on my feet.
But don't look for a rapid recovery
From my wild malignant spree.
Buckle in now for the long run
And remember: "It's all about me!"

I didn't realize until weeks after writing this poem that I had actually psychoanalyzed myself. The real reason I have trouble asking for help is that it feels like I am being this outrageously demanding. The simplest request on my part seems to me an overwhelming burden on others.

Probably all of us err toward one extreme or another—overly demanding or stubbornly independent—and neither serves anyone well. Jesus was the ultimate servant, meeting needs at an exhaustingly sacrificial pace every day of his ministry until his ultimate sacrifice. Yet he offered us the most exquisite examples of being willing to accept service and even to ask for his needs to be met.

Jesus was so gracious in accepting attention and help. Picture him reclining at a dinner table when a woman interrupts to pour oil over his head. In his place I might have been inclined to yell, "What are you doing? You couldn't have chosen a more inappropriate time for this!" But he was neither embarrassed nor inconvenienced. Indeed, when his disciples complained that it was a waste since the money from the expensive oil could have been used to meet the needs of the poor, they seemed to have a valid point! Yet Jesus gallantly defended the woman. I especially love his comment: "She did what she could" (v8). What a simple justification of her actions. I hope on Judgment Day Jesus will say that about me: "Here she is, Father, the one I told you about. I saved her by my blood; she did what she could." That aside, I want to receive the service of others with his graciousness.

He humbly requested a drink of water from a Samaritan woman (John 4:1–26). And then he turned this appeal for her service into an opportunity to offer her living water!

He asked for attendance in his darkest hour. He was so emotionally vulnerable to let his friends watch him struggle through the night before his death—crying, sweating, face in the ground and imploring God for a reprieve—especially when they were so insensitive (Matthew 26:36–46).

In every area of Jesus' life his perfection invites us to imitate. It's easy to discern the enormity of the challenge to be a servant like him, but we might miss the beauty of his humility, graciousness and vulnerability in the ways he accepted help. It a profound lesson God had placed within my reach through his word, but it took some digging around in my beggar's purse to pull it out and make it practical in my life. It is one more example of how completely Jesus surrendered to being human. I want to be that surrendered.

13

PERSPECTIVE

One of faith's greatest challenges is to line our thinking up with God's. After all, he is the one who sees things as they really are and as we should see them. Our thinking gets all muddled with our inclinations, our prejudices, cultural influences and the conclusions we draw from our experiences. But God wants us to become "transformed by the renewing of [our] mind" (Romans 12:1–2). This is a constant challenge for me. Sometimes I think there is nothing that I naturally see the way God sees. It is the ultimate compelling reason I need to go to the Bible regularly to reset my thinking.

Later in Romans 12, we are admonished to "hate what is evil and cling to what is good." God doesn't just want us to *think* the way he does, he also wants us to *feel* the way he does—especially about good and evil. God has emotion, and he longs for us to have emotional intimacy with him by shaping our emotional reactions to match his.

I do not naturally hate the things God hates. I remember

years ago a friend who delighted and amused me. She was feisty, opinionated and outspoken. I found her to be energizing and funny. When a more spiritual sister asked me to help my friend with her pride, I was at first surprised because I had been blind to this sin as the root of my friend's personality. Then I became defensive on her behalf because I didn't want to lose the elements of her character that entertained me. It's much easier for me to point out a sin in someone's life if it is a sin that annoys me. Happily, as my friend grew spiritually, she tempered her opinions with humility, became slower to speak, but retained her charming feistiness.

Similarly, when I first began studying the Bible, I had to face my own pride and tendencies to play the game of one-upmanship with sharp retorts in conversation. I thought it was witty, and I feared that I would be left without any personality if I had to think before I spoke (James 1:19). I often engaged in a competition for the last word; sometimes, the last *cutting* word. My defense: "I was only teasing." I found God had some feelings about that, too:

> Like a madman shooting
>   firebrands or deadly arrows
> is a man who deceives his neighbor
>   and says, "I was only joking." (Proverbs 26:18–19)

It's deceitful to use humor as a cover up for meanness.

My style of humor was certainly not thoughtful of the emotional needs of others. The satisfaction of my own amusement trumped other considerations. Sometimes, if I felt I had lost in a battle of wits, I would actually lose sleep thinking of things I wished I had said! Overcoming these natural inclinations was a blessing for me and everyone around me, and I hate to think what I'd be like now if I'd never seen God's perspective and changed.

Taking every thought captive to Christ (2 Corinthians 10:5) demands that we have some idea of how Christ views things. It's mind-altering work! The only infallible source for the right perspective is the Bible. This is appropriately humbling.

Many tenets of our faith are very clear, and we need to embrace them as the foundation of truth: the existence of God, the Bible as infallible and God-breathed, the plan of salvation, the hope of heaven, the sureness of hell. But most of life leaves room for human judgment, and that's where we need to seek the will of God on our knees. We also need to stay fresh in our search of the Scriptures so we can apply God's truth to every life circumstance. There is a danger in thinking we've *arrived* at all truth; it leaves our Bible study stale if we think we've already figured everything out.

I regularly need to go back to the Bible to find God's

perspective. How should I prioritize my time when demands seem endless? How should I deal with health problems in a spiritual way? How should I regard an enemy? What is a faithful attitude toward finances in an uncertain economy? How should I advise a mother struggling with decisions about child discipline when our culture and her upbringing contradict biblical guidelines? How can I be so in tune with my sinful nature that I can effectively anticipate temptation and avoid it? When should I hold my tongue, and when should I speak?

The list of life circumstances that need to be surrendered to the thinking of God is ongoing. Humility demands that I seek the thinking of God as revealed in his word. This alone will offer a sure path for my faltering, reactionary feet.

> My heart is not proud, O LORD,
>   my eyes are not haughty;
> I do not concern myself with great matters
>   or things too wonderful for me.
> But I have stilled and quieted my soul;
>   like a weaned child with its mother,
>   like a weaned child is my soul within me…
> put your hope in the LORD
>   both now and forevermore. (Psalm 131:1–3)

14

JOY AND HAPPINESS

Years ago I heard a British author (sorry, the name is long lost from my memory) commenting on the American psyche. She observed that Americans say they believe in the right to the pursuit of happiness, but what they really believe in is the right to happiness itself, and if they fail to find it they look for someone to blame. My patriotic self was a little defensive about this assessment, but I had to admit she had a point.

Not long after hearing this stinging portrayal, I saw the movie *Beyond Rangoon*. There is a scene in which an American is explaining her life view to a Buddhist man. Here is a paraphrase of their conversation.

> American woman: "I always believed that if you're good and you work hard, good things will come to you."

> Burmese Buddhist: "We believe that the only promise life keeps is suffering. If something good happens, you should enjoy it for the moment, but do not expect it."

I think it is true that our freedoms in America and the economic system of capitalism have made us believe that we are the masters of our own destinies and that we deserve happiness. Any negative happenstance is often viewed as unfair. We expect prosperity. We also see happiness as produced externally by circumstance rather than internally by decision.

Counter this with the philosophy born in a third-world country where poverty, poor healthcare and class systems enslave many people to life-long hardship, and it becomes understandable that their perspective settles in to a resignation to suffering. There is a certain protection against frustrated hope and disappointment when you expect only misfortune.

But both of these philosophies derive from circumstances. God affirms neither of these viewpoints. While the Bible acknowledges both joy and sorrow as normal life experiences, it offers us transcendence. We live in a fallen world. When sin entered the world, suffering came along as an inseparable companion. Only God gives a universal and timeless solution to the seemingly random and chaotic suffering of man.

God alone offers us explication in the face of destruction. He makes it clear in the Bible that there will be suffering in life, but for those close to him, it will all work out for our best interests. Only faith can ameliorate pain. Two essential ingredients for happiness are *hope* and *gratitude*.

God never intimates that righteousness will be rewarded with a carefree life, but he guarantees that trials will serve a high and holy purpose in our lives. They will make us stronger, teach us perseverance, and mature us spiritually (James 1:2–4). The trick is to value spiritual growth above comfort. That's the secret that makes joy triumph over trials. And it is this secret that gives us hope.

God offers us peace when we face life's "unfair" circumstances—no point in looking for a logical explanation or for someone to blame. Life is unpredictable and misfortune is often random. Jesus took aim at the tendency to try to make sense of human suffering in John 9 when his disciples asked whether the sin of the blind man or his parents had caused his sightlessness. Jesus assured them that neither was to blame for this sad occurrence. God wants us to be free from the frustrating search for why bad things happen and to be at peace in the hopeful knowledge that he will make it turn out for the good.

In addition to hope, God recommends gratitude as a path to happiness. There will never be a human circumstance that can eliminate our reason for gratitude. Even if every earthly comfort is absent, the hope of heaven provides abundant reason for gratitude in the darkest hour. What positive focus could someone summon if they were in physical and emotional agony and had no hope beyond this life? God offers us the ultimate and essential antidote to discouragement and bitterness in Philippians 4:4–8:

> Rejoice in the Lord always. I will say it again: Rejoice! Let your gentleness be evident to all. The Lord is near. Do not be anxious about anything, but in everything, by prayer and petition, with thanksgiving, present your requests to God. And the peace of God, which transcends all understanding, will guard your hearts and minds in Christ Jesus.
>
> Finally, brothers, whatever is true, whatever is noble, whatever is right, whatever is pure, whatever is lovely, whatever is admirable—if anything is excellent or praiseworthy—think about such things.

To be sure, gratitude can be eclipsed by pain. A spirit of gratitude is rarely our default response, but we've seen the people who have hung on to gratitude while coping with hardship, and they become our heroes. It takes decision and focus to capture this joy-producing quality.

In July 2009, I had a second mastectomy that left me with a drain protruding from my right side under my arm. It was uncomfortable and inconvenient. It limited my wardrobe choices and interfered with my sleep. I had high hopes of having it removed at my first doctor's appointment. The deal is that you have to measure the amount of drainage every day, and it has to diminish to a level that your body can absorb before they are willing to remove the long tube and attached bulb.

After week one I was prepared to wait another week to accomplish this removal. At that first appointment the doctor declined to remove the drain, but offered me the great news that there were clean borders around all spots of cancer in my breast, no cancer in the sentinel node they had removed, and I would therefore need no chemo or radiation—truly reason for celebration. I rode an emotional high from this news for several hours after leaving the clinic until the tube rubbing beneath my armpit became annoying, and then I lost the ecstasy.

I had to reclaim my gratitude again and again as it was overshadowed by this minor and temporary trial. Week 2, week 3, week 4, week 5, and the drain was still not ready to be removed. "Hope deferred makes the heart sick" (Proverbs 13:12). A friend said I should give my drain a name. When I shared this idea with my daughter-in-law, she suggested in light of all my moaning that I should name my drain "Mona." I laughed through my shame.

Happiness as a constant is elusive, and sometimes impossible, without a spiritual perspective. We live in a world tragically pursuing a hopeless goal if happiness is dependent on circumstances. And in its pursuit, we find a wake of misery from broken marriages, drug and alcohol abuse, and a myriad of other fruitless efforts to obtain personal joy.

In human reasoning the antidote to disappointed hope is to lower our expectations and settle for the mundane. Until we grow to the point that hope and gratitude are the constant state of our spirits, we will be wise to constantly renew our focus on our blessings on earth and our ultimate hope in heaven. This alone is the hope that will not disappoint (Romans 5:5). Joy in the Lord is the only joy that can never be altered or diminished by life circumstances (1 Thessalonians 5:16).

15

Focus and Priorities

I was a young mother with some compulsions born of post World War II America. When "Johnny [Came] Marching Home," Rosie the Riveter returned from the factories to the hearthside, and the art of homemaking was elevated to sacredness. The new "super-mom syndrome" demanded perfection unattainable by a normal human being.

Retrospectively, it seems milder than the demands of the Martha Stewart era because it didn't throw a career into the equation and stay-at-home motherhood was the norm. Maybe that just proves it wasn't a cultural phenomenon at all, but just a tendency of human nature that will be recycled through every generation. Perhaps there had existed a prehistoric competition among cave wives to have the cleanest caves, the most attractive primitive paintings on the walls and the most succulent wooly mammoth stew recipe. Who knows?

Nevertheless, in the 1960s I was slavishly bound to a self-authored schedule aimed at achieving this ideal. I borrowed some of my self-imposed to-do list from an embroidered set of dish towels, one for each day of the week: Wash on Monday, Iron on Tuesday, Clean on Wednesday, etc. My Tuesday ironing included ironing the sheets. My Wednesday cleaning included moving furniture and scrubbing woodwork—no superficial, sweep-it-under-the-rug slovenliness here!

My self-worth was almost completely tied to how much I accomplished in a day. Disruptions to my routine were anxiety-producing. It threw off my whole week if some unexpected emergency inserted itself into my tidy, packed agenda. I did tend to leave the weekends free of chores and open for spontaneity. But on Fridays, if I found that week's tasks spilling over into the next week's to-do list, I became discouraged with tinges of self-loathing.

I didn't know I needed therapy, and it's just as well because we couldn't have afforded it at the time anyway. You can imagine the impact this had on my relationships, but I was oblivious to that aspect of the problem. Indeed, I was oblivious to acknowledging it as a problem in any form. I thought it was normal, healthy and virtuous, and I clung ever more defensively to that conviction when the women's lib movement began its strident rebellion, trying to free women from that onerous feminine stereotype.

But I was trying to live my life by the teachings of the Bible. The Bible did, indeed, affirm some of my ideas about domestic virtues (see Proverbs 31:10–31 and Titus 2:3–5), but it shattered my priorities, revealing that I valued schedule over people. I could only work in the needs of others if I had two weeks' advance notice to wedge them into my tightly ordered routines. Neither flexibility nor service outside my home was my gift.

I don't remember which passages or circumstances influenced me to take a closer look at the way I ordered my life, but it may have been some of the following:

Romans 12:10 – Be devoted to one another in brotherly love. Honor one another above yourselves.

Galatians 6:9–10 – Let us not become weary in doing good, for at the proper time we will reap a harvest if we do not give up. Therefore, as we have opportunity, let us do good to all people.

Ephesians 5:1–2 – Be imitators of God, therefore, as dearly loved children and live a life of love, just as Christ loved us and gave himself up for us as a fragrant offering and sacrifice to God.

Ephesians 6:7–8 – Serve wholeheartedly, as if you were serving the Lord, not men, because you know that the Lord will reward everyone for whatever good he does.

Titus 3:8b – ...Those who have trusted in God may be
careful to devote themselves to doing what is good.

I was feeling anxious about increasing demands on
my time which, I think, is a natural result of having a
young, growing family. I was also feeling guilty about how
regularly I declined requests for help when others were in
need. One day in what, for me, was a daring pledge, I got
on my knees and promised God I would stop putting my
schedule above people's needs and would not say "no" to
another request just because it inconvenienced me.

Within a week, I was tested on this scary vow. We
lived in San Diego at the time, and I received a phone call
from a young couple whose car had broken down in Los
Angeles. They wanted me to come and pick them up and
bring them back to San Diego. Everything in me wanted
to tell them to try someone else. A sense of panic was rising in me as I thought of the tasks that would have to be
deferred. I imagined the worst-case scenarios of traffic
jams and of my getting lost trying to find them. But I
agreed to go, made the necessary phone calls to readjust
my plans, loaded my kids in the car and headed north. I
literally cried all the way there—it was that hard on me.

Interestingly, traffic was no problem; I drove straight
to them with the directions they had supplied without a
misstep, found them to be overwhelmingly grateful for

my rescue, and we drove home as easily as I had driven there. As far as I know, they had no idea what a reluctant rescuer had come to their aid.

This incident altered my life. My nature remains the same: I thrive on an ordered routine and love a sense of accomplishment, but I rarely panic at disruptions anymore, and my priorities have been turned upside down: people first, schedule second.

Many years later, I found myself doggedly adhering to these priorities more as a philosophical habit than a commitment to a God I loved and trusted. One day I heard my friend Kathy Rosenquist express my needs in her prayer as she asked, "Father, please let my heart catch up with my schedule." It is a prayer I've borrowed many times in the ensuing years.

16

REASONING WITH GOD

When the northern kingdom of Israel embraced idolatry and all the shocking sins that accompanied it, God sent numerous prophets to rebuke, warn and instruct them. It has always fascinated me the way the nature of God is revealed in the appeal of these prophets. While God's rebukes were bitingly stern and his warnings terrifying, they went unheeded. In spite of this, God's expressions of love, his longing to forgive them and his desire to bless them rang loudly above the proclamations of his fury.

The prophet Isaiah is a prime example of this three-pronged outline that nearly every book of prophecy incorporates: (1) repent of your sins, or (2) you'll suffer sure and terrible consequences, but (3) God really loves you and has great blessings in store for your future if you will simply obey him.

Consider how, in the first chapter alone, God rails against their sinfulness:

> Ah, sinful nation,
>> a people loaded with guilt,
> a brood of evildoers,
>> children of corruption!
> They have forsaken the LORD;
>> they have spurned the Holy One of Israel
> and turned their backs on him. (v4)

Then he warns them of the fate that will be theirs if they refuse to repent:

> ...Rebels and sinners will both be broken,
>> and those who forsake the LORD will perish. (v28)

Yet, in the midst of God's completely justified wrath, Isaiah offers this touching invitation:

> "Come now, let us reason together,"
>> says the LORD.
> "Though your sins are like scarlet,
>> they shall be as white as snow;
> though they are red like crimson,
>> they shall be like wool." (v18)

Isaiah wrote extensively warning Israel of the punishment that would be their fate if they failed to repent, and reasoning with them about the justness of God's vengeful response to their depravity. But here God tenderly pleads with them to *come* and *reason* with him, and tells them that he would make it all better if they'd let him.

Webster defines the word "reason" like this: "to think coherently and logically; draw inferences or conclusions from facts known or assumed." You don't have to reason with me too extensively to get me to see that I am a sinner. It makes perfect sense that God should be mad at me. I get it that I don't deserve heaven, and the logical inference is that I do deserve hell! But when I read Isaiah 1:18, I tear up and laugh at the same time.

This is the most unreasonable offer God ever makes! I can't connect the dots here. My sins are scarlet. God is willing to make me as white as snow.

This says nothing about me and everything about God. It is not because I can be sorry enough or good enough or that I can undo any of the myriad things in my life that I bitterly regret. It's about God and a love that longs to set aside his own very justified anger and make me white and pure again. In the exquisitely unfathomable nature of God, mercy triumphs over justice (James 2:13).

This isn't about me reasoning with God and trying to explain or defend myself before him. It's about him reasoning with me to offer what I could not possibly deserve. It's outrageously unreasonable that God should erase my sin. It has nothing to do with my merit and everything to do with his loving and merciful nature. I am eternally grateful for an unreasonable God.

17

STAYING AWAKE

A few years ago, I was reading Luke's account of the transfiguration of Jesus (Luke 9:28–36). It's easy to read the Bible and think you'd respond more spiritually or faithfully than Jesus' disciples did in his presence. Really...think about having Jesus invite you and just two others to join him on a mountainside for prayer. You can imagine yourself to feel honored, alert, almost ethereal, longing to take in every nuance of this special occasion.

As women, we might have carefully mined our closets that day to look appropriate for the occasion—either something with understated elegance or something plain and austere. Tough choices: stilettos and a little black dress or Birkenstocks and muslin? Anyway, there's absolutely no indication that Peter, James or John gave apparel any thought at all. It's pretty clear they considered it a "come as you are" event.

As Luke outlines the developments of the day, we can see the startlingly unique nature of this gathering. First, as Jesus was praying, "the appearance of his face changed."

That might cause some head-turning and heightened attention!

Next, "his clothes became as white as lightening." I don't know if the custom of closing your eyes in prayer was already in place, which could excuse their failure to notice his face changing, but even with your eyes closed, you'd notice sustained lightning and open them to see what was going on.

Then "Moses and Elijah appeared in glorious splendor." This surely was an incomparable happening and a unmistakable clue that careful attention was warranted. Perhaps they did not immediately recognize Moses and Elijah since they had died many years earlier, but considering the Bible's tendency for understatement, this "glorious splendor" thing had to be a real tip-off that these two guys were prominent figures.

Plus, the next thing Luke reveals to us is that Jesus, Moses and Elijah began chatting about "his departure, which he was about to bring to fulfillment at Jerusalem"—no ordinary topic! He's talking about his death and ascension—what a conversation to overhear!

But here's the funny part: After this spectacular sequence of events, the next verse says, "Peter and his companions were very sleepy, but when they became fully awake, they saw his glory and the two men standing with him." There is no way to exaggerate the exalted glory of this scene. At first glance I started laughing out loud at the dullness of the disciples. They are witnesses to one of the most magnificent, sensational moments in the history of the world, and these guys are yawning and rubbing the sleep from their eyes!

Peter finally senses it's time for an appropriately impressive response, so he gives it his best shot with: "'Master it's good for us to be here. Let us put up three shelters ["shrines" in the New Living Translation]—one for you, and one for Moses and one for Elijah.' (He did not know what he was saying.)" No kidding! The first verse of this chapter lets us know that this event occurred just eight days after Peter had proclaimed, "You are the Christ, the Son of the living God!" That's when he *really* didn't know what he was saying because if he'd understood the implications of that statement, he'd have never placed Jesus on the same level as Moses and Elijah and thought to honor them equally with their own little individual tabernacles. What a guy—always ready to jump in with both feet…and then stick one in his mouth.

So, without Jesus even getting a chance to reply, his Father finally couldn't take it any longer, and they heard his voice from a cloud: "THIS IS MY SON…."

Finally, Luke tells us that "the disciples kept this to

themselves, and told no one at that time what they had seen." Either they were too embarrassed to admit to their somnambulant dullness, or they figured no one would believe such an outrageous story anyway.

I stopped laughing when it started dawning on me that this remarkable story graphically reveals the dullness to which I'm susceptible as well. While I can see that there's no excuse for these three taking for granted an invitation from the Son of God to go pray with him, I often get ready for church in distracted habitual routine, ungrateful for the amazing privilege and unprepared to make the most of it.

Worse yet, on really unspiritual days, I can become an evaluator of the worship experience offered to me rather than a grateful, fully engaged participant. I can sing the songs and hear the sermon, even take notes, with blasé detachment. I can fight for concentration during communion instead of being riveted by the thought of Jesus' unspeakable sacrifice. I can drop my check into the offering plate and feel a tinge of reluctance to part with the money instead of wishing I could give more because of all that God has given to me, and the remarkable privilege of offering him anything.

God wants us fully awake! He wants us to experience every moment of our lives with the exuberant joy of having our sins forgiven and having a purpose in life that trumps every other human endeavor. He wants us to approach the assembly of the body enraptured by the privilege of getting to unite our hearts with our brothers and sisters to express our devotion to him. He wants us to sing with all our hearts, thrilled to ring out our praises to him and to inspire one another. He wants us to pray filled with awe that we can amplify the power of our prayers when we unite our hearts (Colossians 3:15–17).

And isn't that what we all want? To live our lives with joy, energy, hope and purpose? Don't we want every day to have meaning, discovery and adventure? This is what God offers us with a life in Jesus! My musing over these parallels in first-century inclinations and twenty-first century inclinations inspired the following lyrics:

Wake Up the World

An exclusive invitation brought three followers to
the mount
Unprepared for the wonders they would see.
And their sleepy eyes, unfocused, were delayed in
catching sight
Of their Lord transfigured by eternity.

Lord, please wake us up to your glory.
Lift the veil that dims our view.
Use our words and our lives to tell the story

That will make your dreams come true.

Now a groggy world moves blindly through a sin-
    infested haze
With a Father who is watching from above,
And longing for his children in this world to be his
    voice,
Longing to be known for his love.

We will wake up the world to his glory,
Lift the veil that dims their view,
And our words and our lives will tell the story—
Working to make God's dreams come true.

Still, a risen Savior calls us to be transformed by his
    truth,
And our prayer is that every man will hear,
And every eye be opened to the power of offered
    hope
As the day of his return is drawing near.

We will wake up the world to his glory,
Lift the veil that dims their view,
And our words and our lives will tell the story—
Working to make God's dreams come true.

I long to be awake every day to the joy of a relationship with God. I want to be alert to the efforts of Satan to
steal my joy. I've found that people who try to live out

godly principles from a sense of duty instead of delight lose their motivation and burn out. This is why Psalm 119 is so profound. In every way possible, David articulated his freedom and delight in the commands of God.

It's often easy at the beginning of your Christian walk to be overcome with joy and gratitude, but to have to work at it as time goes on. It is similar to the difference between infatuation and love. Infatuation sweeps you off your feet and consumes you, but as that initial rush turns into the commitment of love, it shifts from being controlled by an external force to taking control of an internal force. Maintaining and building a love relationship involves remaining in awe of your beloved, staying aware and grateful for his blessings, and rejoicing in all that he is and all that he offers.

If we can stay awake to the wonder of God and his promises, we'll stay head-over-heals in love, and we'll find the same vivacious endurance as the recipients of Peter's first letter when he told them,

> Though you have not seen him, you love him; and even though you do not see him now, you believe in him and are filled with an inexpressible and glorious joy, for you are receiving the goal of your faith, the salvation of your souls. (1 Peter 1:8–9)

18

ONE DAY AT A TIME

When our son Greg was three or four years old, he began evidencing a trait that was at once amusing and frustrating to us. We could be at Disneyland on the ride of a lifetime, and in the middle of the ecstasy he would ask, "What are we going to do next?" or "What are we doing tomorrow?" My standard reply was, "I don't know! Enjoy what we're doing now!" I even wrote a little song that I would sing to him:

> Don't spend all your hopes on tomorrow, my son.
> Tomorrow's a prize that is yet to be won,
> But this day you hold in your hand—
> Its wonders are at your command.
>
> Be still and alert, my son; watch the grass grow,
> Smell warm summer mornings, and feel winter's
> snow.
> Impatience will soon make you blind
> To treasures you'd otherwise find.
>
> So offer fresh popcorn to birds in the park.

Love daylight as well as its fading to dark.
Take each chance that happens your way
To taste of the joy in today.

Working through this with Greg did little to increase my own awareness that it was a characteristic he had probably inherited from me! The first time I became keenly aware of my own difficulty with living one day at a time was in 1982 when Ron was diagnosed with cancer. We had four children ages eleven to eighteen years old, and I battled daily the fears of what I would do if I had to raise them alone. I indulged in horrifying scenes of what lay ahead in the months I might have to watch Ron suffer through chemotherapy and/or death. I worried about our children being without a father; I worried about finances, home maintenance, loneliness, my identity without Ron and dozens of other unpleasant possibilities. I found myself unable to be what Ron and my children needed me to be in the present because I was consumed with the uncertainties of the future.

I realized that when things were going well, I made plans for tomorrow as if tomorrow were guaranteed. I love feeling that my future is predictable. This fallacy can make me quite independent from God. Hard times drive me to my knees, begging God to fix what I cannot, yet I still try to picture the future and come up with solutions for alternate circumstances. Ron's cancer confirmed my impotence.

Our situation had a happy ending: Ron was cured with radiation therapy, and we raised our family together. Before I knew the outcome, I didn't know what sorrow or hardship might lie ahead, but I knew it wouldn't be forever. Ron would either get well or he would die, and in the meantime, there was a faith and hope and joy that God was calling me to. Either way, I had a limited time to rise to the occasion. Changing my outlook to others-centered compassion instead of self-centered fears was the only way I could contribute positively to a negative situation. I knew that after the crisis, no matter the outcome, I would have fewer regrets if I became what Ron and our kids needed me to be.

I knew of Jesus' admonishment: "Therefore do not worry about tomorrow, for tomorrow will worry about itself. Each day has enough trouble of its own" (Matthew 6:34). I tried to "repent" of this sin of worry, but it haunted my subconscious even in my sleep, and I felt like an unwilling victim of my own dark imagination. I think repentance is not so much the issue here as "being transformed by the renewing of your mind" (Romans 12:2).

We are created by God with some limitations common to human nature. We are not designed to take on

much more than our current circumstances. God alone
can deal practically and emotionally with unlimited problems. Since we do not know the future, we overwhelm
ourselves emotionally and stunt our growth spiritually
when we borrow tomorrow's multitude of ill-conceived
eventualities. It is truly more than we can bear.

Current vernacular encourages us to "live in the present" as if it's a wisdom newly articulated by an enlight-
ened generation. Amazing how we take ancient truths
from God and repackage them to pretend they are our
own! In James 4:13–14, we are cautioned:

> Now listen, you who say, "Today or tomorrow we will
> go to this or that city...." Why, you do not even know
> what will happen tomorrow. What is your life? You
> are a mist that appears for a little while and then
> vanishes.

It was this scripture that informed my new mindset. I
forced myself several times a day (as fears demanded my
attention) to go through this little exercise: "What do I
know today? Today I know Ron is alive. Today I know he
and my children need me to be happy and hopeful. I know
how to do those things for today. I don't know about tomorrow, but I know that God knows, and he will give me the
strength, wisdom and spiritual counselors to help me deal
with tomorrow. I will focus on today." It may sound corny,

but this little exercise was my sanity during that period and became the drill I returned to during future trials.

I don't maintain this positive way of thinking natural-ly. It is still my nature to worry about tomorrow. I return to this mindset by decision and with much effort, but it does have a transforming power. In my youth, I actually envisioned myself growing into a wise and serene spiritu-al maturity that would be little short of legendary. I thought wisdom and peace would exude from every wrinkle and gray hair. I have been disappointed to discov-er that peaceful sagacity did not come to me with age— the saying on the birthday card is true: "They say with age comes wisdom…sometimes age just comes alone." All the things I didn't like about myself at twenty-five are pretty much the things I still don't like about myself. I just have a few more God-supplied tools in my beggar's purse to deal with them.

The world will always offer us reasons to borrow tomorrow's problems. Now that I'm finished raising my children, I remain vulnerable to worry over them as well as their children: their health, their faith, their jobs and their general happiness. Plus, there is the economy, terrorism, our retirement fund and the spiritual health of the church-es. There is no end to the list if we are given to worry.

In 2006, my doctors found a mass in my left lung

about the size of a baseball. This produced an annoying, persistent cough, compromised my breathing and made it hard for me to sleep comfortably through the night. One morning after this discovery, and while a biopsy had still not revealed a diagnosis, I groggily surfaced from slumber to find myself wheezing and breathing with some effort. In this half-awake state, I went to the bad place in my mind. I moaned and wondered how agonizing it would be to lie for days on my death bed, gasping for breath.

I finally became fully awake enough to re-embrace my old one-day-at-a-time decision. I laughed thinking to myself: And *if* I *do* die a horrible, oxygen-deprived death, I'll look back on this day and say, "I felt *great* that day! I can't believe I wasted it dreading this one!" (In the meantime, I have been diagnosed and have moved into remission with non-Hodgkin's lymphoma, which presented in the lymphatic tissue of my left lung rather than in lymph nodes as it typically does.)

I wish I were further along in my faith and wisdom. I wish worry were now a distant memory of my immature past. The truth is, I am as prone to worry about insignificant things as about big things. I think it is sometimes easier for me to let go of the big things since I know I cannot control them, yet fret about the little things over which I maintain an illusion of control.

Apparently, somewhere in the recesses of my mind, I believe that if I spend enough time agonizing over a problem, I will eventually come up with a perfect solution. Silly me! Paul said, "I can do everything through him who gives me strength" (Philippians 4:13). Somehow, buried deep within my psyche is the idea that I can do all things if I just brood about them long enough! Foolish arrogance!

Taking one day at a time is the only sure way to deal with responsibilities that are ours while leaving the rest to God. It's a great way to live. I think God tells us not to worry to protect us rather than to scold us. He's trying to offer us both sanity and peace. I like the saying: "I don't know what the future holds, but I know who holds the future."

19

RUNNING ON EMPTY

Nearly every experience in life can teach us something about ourselves and, if we are tuned in, something about God. Many years ago, I was going through a particularly dark period. I don't even recall the circumstances that had accumulated to put me in such a pit, but I do remember the feelings of despair. In particular, I felt very disconnected from God, as if he were not hearing my prayers or caring about my situation. I wasn't blaming this on him. I was very down on myself at the time and felt he was ignoring me with total justification.

In this condition of self-loathing and emotional fatigue, I was still plodding through my daily routines, which included beginning my day with Bible reading. Mostly this was a numbing exercise, and my inspiration and retention level were at an all-time low. You may wonder why I didn't run to the nearest doctor for a prescription for antidepressants. It didn't occur to me. I didn't know that I was depressed. I thought I was simply living within the very rational assessment of my own worthlessness and felt helpless to alter that perception, but increasingly disheartened by it until one day I read Isaiah 55:

> "Come, all you who are thirsty,
>   come to the waters;
> and you who have no money,
>   come buy and eat!
> Come, buy wine and milk
>   without money and without cost....
> Listen, listen to me, and eat what is good,
>   and your soul will delight in the richest of fare."
> (vv1–2)

This resonated with me in a profoundly hopeful way. I felt emotionally and spiritually bankrupt; hungry, yet without the energy to lift a cup to my mouth. But here was God, reassuring me that my bankruptcy was a non-issue. He would supply my needs without me having anything to offer in return. I think it felt especially relevant that he didn't say, "...And you who have no money, come and I'll just give it to you for free." While in one sense this is true, I needed the very words he chose to know that what I was being offered wasn't a low-budget welfare meal. It's the best there is—an expensive, gourmet feast that God wants me to buy without money. Why does he use the word "buy" if it's free? What is the currency that I exchange for this life-saving sustenance?

It is found in the word "come." I come empty-handed,

but I come, and that is enough for God. He just wants me to come—and in that coming to proclaim my dependence, my trust, my awareness of my own inadequacy to meet my most urgent needs.

What does it mean to come? For one thing, it means acknowledging the presence of God by talking to him. But the kind of prayers I was accustomed to praying seemed hollow and hypocritical at that time. So my efforts at prayer in those days ran along these lines: "God, I don't want to pray right now, and I don't know what to ask for, but I know you are the only one I can turn to. Please help me." That was the best I could seem to do. It was enough for God.

Additionally, reading the Bible felt like a futile exercise, but my decision to "come" included a decision to come to his word. I may as well have been reading the phone book for all the spiritual insight I seemed to be getting out of it, but verses 10–12 in Isaiah 55 made me wearily decide to test this wonderful promise of God:

> As the rain and the snow
>   come down from heaven,
> and do not return to it
>   without watering the earth
> and making it bud and flourish,
>   so that it yields seed for the sower and bread for
>   the eater,

so is my word that goes out from my mouth:
   It will not return to me empty,
but will accomplish what I desire
   and achieve the purpose for which I sent it.
You will go out in joy
   and be led forth in peace;
the mountains and hills
   will burst into song before you,
and all the trees of the field
   will clap their hands.

This seemed like a pretty exuberant promise for someone as down as I was, but I had nothing to lose in giving it a try. Nothing in these verses suggested that the Bible's effectiveness depended on my mood or ability to concentrate. I let go of the quiet fear and frustration that I was stuck in a downward spiral and settled into a routine of prayer and Bible reading while waiting for God to transform my spirit.

I was depressed enough that this level of discipline was a daily challenge for me, but I forced myself to stick with the routine, and it ultimately proved to be a turning point. In a matter of a few weeks, Isaiah 55 became the branch at the edge of the cliff that I clung to and that God eventually used to pull me up onto solid ground again. I began looking up to the generous power of God to supply life and hope and purpose and joy.

Years later this experience sprang to mind again when

I heard a friend remark, "Sometimes we try to get the strength to go to God instead of going to God for the strength."

Reading on in chapter 55 of Isaiah, I learned the futility of the obsessive, negative self-analysis I'd been engaging in. There was no way of thinking myself out of my troubled perspective. The world often counsels us to look within ourselves to find answers. This has limited value given the sordid early experiences of many of our lives. Even more foolish is the pseudo-spiritual admonition to "find the God within yourself." Believe me, naturally speaking, he's not there! When we shape God into an image fitting our concept of what deity should look like, that god embodies all of our prejudices, misconceptions, weaknesses and an unhealthy dose of our wildest dreams. Collectively, then, we end up with a polytheistic group of warring gods answering to their basest natures.

Sound familiar? Think Greek mythology. There is no place to find God except in the places he has revealed himself. Isaiah 55 confirms this in verses 6–8:

> Seek the LORD while he may be found....
> Let the wicked forsake...his thoughts....
>
> "For my thoughts are not your thoughts,
>   neither are my ways your ways ,"
> declares the LORD.

Wisdom and humility demand that we pay less attention to our own thinking than to God's. While I knew this on a rational level, on an emotional level during this shadowed period of my life, I seemed unable to escape my negativity. Yet through God's mercy and power, he spoke directly to my heart in Isaiah 55 and restored my soul.

20

GENERATIONAL SINS

Peter's warning to the crowd gathered on Pentecost in Acts 2 to "save yourselves from this corrupt generation" has timeless relevance. There is a corruption common to every age and every culture. Paul told the Galatians that Christ had died for our sins "to rescue us from the present evil age," and appealed to the Ephesians to "be careful…because the days are evil."

Paul stereotyped the sins of the people of Crete: "Even as one of their own prophets has said, 'Cretans are always liars, evil brutes, lazy gluttons'" (Titus 1:12). While this may appear to us to be shockingly politically incorrect (probably because of our own cultural sins), God has never hesitated to generalize the sins of a group of people. Does it make you wonder what he would say about us in the twenty-first century? He does have an opinion about us, I assure you.

Perhaps he would call us a generation of disrespect. It's easy to become numb to attitudes that permeate our airwaves. Sassy, insolent remarks from children to parents have become a common form of movie and TV comedy. Youthful crudeness and profanity are often regarded as amusingly precocious rather than offensive.

Maybe he would address our blasé acceptance of immorality. Sex reserved for marriage is seen as archaic, illogical, intolerant, puritanical and even unwise. As we have drifted away from God's plan, our attitudes have adjusted to accommodate our cultural lifestyles. Refusing to acknowledge that we have become amoral, we instead have created a morality on our own terms. For instance, rather than calling abortion a sin, our culture is more likely to decry denying a woman the freedom to murder her unborn child. We have a new standard for moral outrage, and it stands in opposition to God's standard.

It is tragic that, while rejecting God's view of what is right and wrong, we dare to substitute a moral code of our own construction. We no longer look to God to determine good and evil, but to ourselves. This is arrogant humanism run amok. While this reveals a God-instilled hunger in the soul of man for a standard by which to measure morality, it also reveals the way Satan seeks to hijack our best inclinations and distort them for his purposes.

Perhaps there has never been a generation so godly that Isaiah's admonition to Israel was inapplicable, but it has never been more appropriately applied than it is to us today:

Woe to those who call evil good
    and good evil,
who put darkness for light
    and light for darkness,
who put bitter for sweet
    and sweet for bitter. (Isaiah 5:20)

As a grandmother of ten, I'm concerned about the world my grandchildren will inherit. Six of the ten are already teens, and I see the complexity of the issues they have to navigate in order to find clear convictions of their own. Jesus' parable of the sower has powerful application for this age group (Matthew 13:1–23). In this familiar and profound allegory, he reveals four conditions of the human heart to which the word of God is offered.

Probably every human being has patches of each kind of soil in their hearts, some more prominent than others depending on their individual natures and life circumstances. In pursuing a relationship with God we all have to cultivate our hearts to become good soil that can be deeply affected by truth. But it seems in our current culture, teens have an overwhelming mingling of all four soils to sort through in order to settle on a faith of their own.

Jesus describes the first heart-condition as being hard, like a well-trodden path. Here is Satan's greatest hope: that our kids will have hearts with no ability to absorb

God's word. He wants them to be skeptical and resistant to truth either because of disillusionment or the appeal of sin.

Temptation has never been more culturally pervasive—it streams into our homes on cables through TV and the Internet twenty-four hours a day, and our government and school systems pointedly seek to indoctrinate our children to accept sin as the norm. They are made to feel guilty, petty, backward and prejudiced if they embrace God's view of evil. The Bible warns us to avoid behavior that is "evil in the eyes of the Lord." (Look through 2 Kings 21–24 and see how many times God condemns the kings of Israel because "they did evil in the eyes of the Lord.") He could have simply said "they did evil," but he specifically notes that it was *his* standard they broke.

In our current culture we are prone to be intimidated by things deemed evil in the eyes of man—afraid to wear a fur coat or admit we bow to God's condemnation of homosexuality. The world now seems to place greater moral value on animal rights and recycling than on the commands of God. As the creation has dared to rebel against the Creator, we are living out Romans 1:18–32.

The second soil relates to rocky terrain where the soil is shallow. What could better describe the hormonal ups and downs of teenagers? Their passionate enchantment one day is replaced by disdain the next. How Satan must love youthful inconsistencies! He surely plays on these ebbs and flows to make a sustainable focus or an unshakable commitment a very difficult task for them. Satan is skilled beyond our wildest nightmares at introducing trouble and persecution into the lives of teens. At just the stage of life where acceptance from peers matters the most, Satan makes a godly lifestyle appear to be social suicide.

Then there is the thorny soil—if thorns are worries, who has more thorns than teens? They worry about their grades, their complexions, their popularity, their futures, their school assignments, their schedules, their parents' unreasonableness, their wardrobes, their emerging identities, and their success at academics, sports and life in general. Satan works overtime to choke out every spiritual impulse with worry.

Last is the good soil—the pure heart that has no obstructions to prohibit internalizing and responding to the word of God. This is the soil we covet for ourselves and everyone we love! Most teens who have had the moral advantage of being raised by Christian parents have abundant good soil and the fertilizer of youthful zeal to overcome the three-to-one odds. So Satan doesn't have the upper hand, but he has more influence than we can be comfortable with. What is the adult role in helping our teens circumvent this quagmire?

Love them. Have compassion for the struggles they face. Believe in them. Praise them for every good quality and deed. Set a great example for them. Listen to them. Talk to them (instead of preach). Be honest with them, "speaking the truth in love" (Ephesians 4:15). Set clear, fair and defensible boundaries with appropriate consequences. Pray for them. Assist them in their study of the Bible by your own excitement and discovery from your time in the Word.

Encourage, comfort and urge them to live lives worthy of the God who is calling them into his kingdom and glory (1 Thessalonians 2:12). Sacrifice for them to be part of every wholesome, Bible-centered activity offered. Make it possible for them to spend time with other families and teens who share your beliefs. Solicit the interest of other Christian adults in their lives. Delight in them. Make Christianity fun.

I do not claim that Ron and I did this perfectly with our own four kids. Their teen years presented many challenges, but perhaps not as great as their children are facing. Our culture is moving further and further from God, yet we must not stand by as if helpless. There is a world to be won to Jesus for the sake of each soul saved and the hope of the next generation:

> We will not hide them from their children;
>   we will tell the next generation
> the praiseworthy deeds of the Lord,
>   his power, and the wonders he has done.
>
> ...so the next generation would know them,
>   even the children yet to be born,
>   and they in turn would tell their children.
> (Psalm 78:4, 6)

21

JUDGING GOD

I am confident that coming to know God—mining out the infinite intricacies of his divine nature—is a lifetime process and ends with us only having skimmed the surface. In seeking God we are attempting to search out multifaceted perfection from a vantage point that has no associative counterpart. But we try, oh, we try to explain the nature and thinking of God based on the circumstances of our life.

It is perhaps both in my nature and my earliest religious experiences to feel accused and guilty. These inclinations toward self-reproach make it very easy to assume that God is as disappointed, even furious, with me as I am with myself when I sin. Therefore, unchecked by the truths of the Bible, I imagine God to be accusing and quick to turn his back in disgust on the errant mortal—mostly if it is me; I have a lot more grace for others. I also see him as justified in outrage and vengeance (both of which he has the capacity for), but I tend to see his wrath as being untempered by the overriding truth that in his heart "mercy triumphs over judgment" (James 2:13). He is also understanding and compassionate: "...he remembers that we are dust" (Psalm 103:13–14). And ultimately, his boundless love for us makes him so eager to forgive us that he let his Son die to make it possible!

For me, however, it is a surrendering of my intellect to the truth of Scripture and displacing my innate emotional bent, that enables me to accept him as he says he is and has proven himself to be.

I share all this only to offer a personal illustration of how our own perspectives can cause us to misconceive God. I think the universe cannot hold a more tragic distortion than a misrepresentation of the nature of our Creator, Sustainer and Savior. Perhaps it is Satan's greatest ploy. Unless we have a basically accurate view of the nature of God, we will distort his will for our lives and his commands because both can only be deeply understood in light of who he is. So many people dismiss much of the Bible because a loving God, by their definition of love, could not have meant what he said when promising there would be consequences for sin (Galatians 6:7–8).

I was approached once by a woman to debate a particular religious doctrine (the end of time and judgment). Her concept of Jesus was, in my mind, nothing short of blasphemous. I told her I would not look at the Scripture with her on her chosen topic until we had studied out John 8 together to agree on who Jesus is (particularly referencing John 8:58, where he emphatically states that he is the I Am). She declined, but I stand by my reasoning: What does it matter what he taught unless we know who he is and that he has the authority to dictate the standards by which we live—whether we understand them and agree with them or not?

It boils down to judging God. Imagine such smug presumption that we would dare to pass judgment on God! But I do it, too. It probably happens in more hearts than not; this is not arrogance restricted to pagans.

I have long believed that the book of Job is not so much a poetic treatise on bad things happening to good people, as an exposé of how erroneous human perspective is when we judge God by our circumstances. His word alone can reveal unclouded truth regarding who he is.

Job and his friends were spiritual people. It is truly touching that Job's friends "set out from their homes and met together by agreement to go and sympathize with him and comfort him" (Job 2:11). They even wept aloud upon seeing him and didn't even speak for the first seven days. Job was the one who finally broke the silence—no telling how long they would have stayed and remained mute if he hadn't spoken up. In response to Job's initial

lament, Eliphaz betrays the source of his perspective in
Job 4:8–9:

> "As I have observed, those who plow evil
>   and those who sow trouble reap it.
> At the breath of God they are destroyed;
>   at the blast of his anger they perish."

What a dagger in Job's heart to find that his friends
believed he deserved what he got in the loss of his family,
his possessions and his health! But they were not just
standing in judgment of Job; they were standing in judgment of God as well. Job's friends had based their judgment of the nature and actions of God on their observa-
tions of life.

This misjudgment of the workings of God is a common human oversimplification of right and wrong, blessings and punishment. Jesus' friends were prone to this
kind of faulty reasoning, too. In John 9, upon encountering a blind man, Jesus' disciples asked him: "Rabbi, who
sinned, this man or his parents, that he was born blind?"
And Jeremiah complained to God that he seemed to be
showering blessings on the wrong recipients:

> You are always righteous, O LORD,
>   when I bring a case before you.
> Yet I would speak with you about your justice:
>   Why does the way of the wicked prosper?

Why do all the faithless live at ease?
(Jeremiah 12:1)

It's a little shocking to find a prophet of God questioning God's fairness! But I have to confess the great comfort I find in God's tolerating such inappropriate boldness. He is a patient God, indeed—a quality I'm banking on in light of all my many regrettable declarations from time to time.

Job, too, passed judgment on the justice of God. He considered God to have made a mistake because he saw himself as, if not completely innocent, then at least good enough to be unworthy of such severe punishment. How easy it is to entertain this illusion of righteousness! Most of us will admit we're not perfect, but we claim to be "good" people. Our definition of goodness is graded with a bell curve while God's definition of goodness is absolute—untainted good, not mostly good or comparatively good. The standard by which we assess our own righteousness is not the same as God's. The truth is, we have no right to create a standard at all, and are best advised to spend our energies trying to know and apply the standard of God to our lives in great humility.

Both Job and his friends tried to judge the thinking of God relative to the circumstances Job was encountering. From his friends' rationale, God would only let such tragedy befall someone who deserved the punishment;

from Job's rationale, God had been unfair in the extreme. Job didn't claim to be sinless, but he did claim that his sins weren't bad enough to warrant such an agonizing fate (Job 7:20–21). God's permitting Job to suffer had nothing to do with Job deserving it or not. Both Job and his friends judged wrongly, and God cleared up their confusion resoundingly with his response in chapters 38–41. I hesitantly offer the following summarized paraphrase: "Do you know who I am? Would you presume to correct me?"

Job's reply to God was appropriately contrite. God had patiently endured abundant defamation in the conversation between Job and his friends before God came to his own defense.

We can never know God by evaluating our own experiences or our own insecurities. It is a laughably tragic misconception that we might find God by looking within ourselves. A remarkably loving, patient and humble God has entrusted us with knowledge of himself. Both in his word and in the life of his Son, he has poured his heart into helping us understand him, all the while knowing that the closest we would ever come to conceiving of his greatness, his holiness and his mercy would amount to little more than an insult. Yet he loves our efforts to know and to love him, though the worship and praise we offer him could never approach his worth.

Hoping not to stretch a self-constructed analogy too far, I would offer that it is important to try to keep our beggar's purses free of our own ideas and pure in their content of truth from God. We may have to sort through the contents from time to time as we accumulate what seems to be from God, measuring it against God's inspired word or learning through prayerful experience and godly input that we misunderstood or misapplied truth. Above all, it is important not to construct our image of God based on our life experiences, but on God revealing himself to us through his word.

I think this must be why God sets us in families and uses those most intimate and devoted associations to describe our relationship to him. He calls himself our Father! And he explains the extent of his love for us in words and in action:

> How great is the love the Father has lavished on us, that we should be called the children of God! And that is what we are! (1 John 3:1a)

My youngest and most geographically distant grandchild is also, perhaps, the most sentimental. Because of the expense and inconvenience of travel, I don't get to see him very often. On a recent visit he came to me with a crayon-drawn self-portrait, offering it up to me with sad eyes, saying, "This is so you won't forget me." My heart almost broke at the idea that he could even entertain the thought that I might forget him! I considered all day how I could reassure him. It occurred to me that I could not really pledge to never forget him because if, like my mother, I ever suffer from Alzheimer's, I might, indeed, forget him and everyone else.

At the end of the day, I wrote him this poem (and then realized it applied to all my grandchildren and children, as well):

> And what's the chance that I'd forget you?
> What are the odds you'd slip my mind?
> A fragile mind could lose its bearings—
> Your image in my heart I'd find.
> Could the dawn forget the morning?
> Could the moon forget the sun?
> You'll remain within my mem'ry
> Even when my life is done.
> I'll carry you into forever,
> Watching you, though from afar,
> Rejoicing in your ev'ry triumph.
> Delighting in all that you are.

Days later I realized that perhaps a little unintention-al plagiarism was involved in this poetic offering when I remembered God's similar declaration of love in Isaiah 49:15–16:

> "Can a mother forget the baby at her breast
>> And have no compassion on the child she has
>>> borne?
> Though she may forget,
>> I will not forget you!
> See, I have engraved you on the palms of my hands;
>> your walls are ever before me."

Were it not for the love of God, we would not even know what love is (1 John 3:16). It must surely cause pain to the heart of God when we negatively judge the quality, quantity or endurance of his amazing love for us.

22

DISPUTES

When God founded his new nation under the leadership of Moses, he established the organizational system that would define their holiness and heritage. Close on the heels of the Ten Commandments (the premier, foundational laws of righteousness for the Jewish nation) a variety of other laws were enacted to guarantee civility. Early in the list was a plan to deal with their disputes. But even before they reached Sinai, Moses was so busy with this ministry of resolution that his father-in-law was worried about him. He recommended that Moses spread this task among other capable men so that only the most difficult cases would come to Moses (Exodus 18:13–26).

In the idealistic fellowship-fantasy of Christians, we can assume there is something wrong if we have disputes. Disputes are not wrong; they are inevitable simply because we are human. The only thing wrong is allowing disputes to go unresolved. God understands and, through his law, helps us to understand the importance of resolution efforts.

It's a little surprising to see in the Bible how much attention is given to this problem of human disputes. After leaving Egypt, the first time that Moses left the people without his leadership was when he went up to Mt. Sinai to meet with God. He left Aaron and Hur in charge specifically so that "anyone involved in a dispute [could] go to them" (Exodus 24:14). Imagine that! The likelihood of conflicts that could not be resolved without intervention was so predictable that Moses made careful preparation in advance. It would be comforting to think that we've matured beyond this tendency or that the Israelites were just uncommonly contentious, but, no; it is still a problem common to man.

Occasionally I am called upon to meet with two women who have hit an impasse in their attempts to overcome hurt feelings, conflicts of convictions (interesting how two God-loving, Bible-loving people can see exactly the same circumstance from completely different angles), unmet expectations, and a variety of other joy- and unity-destroying events. Paul told the Ephesian church to "make every effort to keep the unity of the Spirit in the bond of peace" (Ephesians 4:3). I think he said this because it really does take "every effort." We can't just rely on having the same understandings in our beggar's purses to prevent different points of view.

Still I often find women dismayed and embarrassed, reluctant to enter into the resolution process, and skeptical that resolution is possible. Surely one reason the Bible records disputes is for us to learn how to regard them. Can you imagine being in church the Sunday morning the disciples in Philippi received the letter from their beloved apostle Paul? Think how eager everyone was to get news from him, to be taught by him again. They must have been on the edge of their seats.

And what an encouraging letter it was—his vulnerability in expressing his love for them, his confidence in their faith, his reassurances that he was thriving spiritually in spite of being imprisoned, his inspiring instructions about humility, obedience, shining like stars, growth and perseverance—and then he throws in a personal concern about a disagreement between Euodia and Syntyche! He didn't expose the nature of the dispute. He didn't take sides. He praised them both and simply asked that others love them enough to get involved and help them.

I've been on both sides of the table in this. I recall feeling misunderstood by a friend and feeling frustrated that I could not make her see my position to my satisfaction. She, on the other hand, felt I was being stubborn and prideful in failing to accept her assessment of the situation which, in turn, made me feel unfairly judged. Our efforts to resolve this with one another just dug the hole deeper. We finally agreed to solicit the helpful intervention of a mutual friend.

This can feel risky. Satan wants us to fear that the problem will grow more painfully complex instead of being happily resolved. He can stir up fears that the mediator with be partial, taking sides against us. We can fear looking foolish. I guess all this could happen, but I've only experienced fair and impartial help that opened my eyes to my own misperceptions and clarified my position for the friend with whom I had the conflict in an objective and non-emotional way.

Yet, the truth is, God understands that not every conflict will have an immediately satisfying ending. Think of Paul, John Mark and Barnabas in Acts15:36–41, where we're told they "had such a sharp disagreement that they parted company." How painful: a triangular impasse with no apparent effective mediator! Yet, again, the Bible gives us no clue that one was right and the other wrong. We often surmise that Paul was the one favored by God because the Bible story continues detailing Paul's ministry, not that of Barnabas and John Mark, but we really don't know for sure. There could be lots of other reasons God chose to follow Paul and his other companions in the biblical account of spreading the gospel.

We do get the encouraging sense that hard feelings did not end their relationship because in 2 Timothy 4:11, near the end of Paul's life, he asks for John Mark to come to him "because he is helpful to me in my ministry."

Our sense of justice can be offended by the admonition in Proverbs that "a man's wisdom gives him patience; it is to his glory to overlook an offense" (Proverbs 19:11). I am always a little awestruck by Paul's instruction to the Corinthians (1 Corinthians 6:1–11) about cheating and wrongdoing that was serious enough to be heard in a civil court. He assures them that disciples are competent judges in such matters. So much for the notion that we need someone with a degree in criminal justice! Spiritual wisdom will always outrank worldly wisdom no matter how learned, erudite and sophisticated. But the part that stuns me a bit and calls me to the high road is his ultimate argument that it is such a shameful thing to go to civil court against a brother that it is better to be wronged, better to be cheated.

I know my own sinful nature and the struggle I would have going to church Sunday after Sunday, having communion after communion, with someone who (in my opinion) had swindled me and having to learn to deal with the bitterness that I'd be vulnerable to. I'd have to learn love and forgiveness at a level that challenges my very core! Maybe verse 9 is there to reassure us that ulti-mately they won't get away with it if they don't repent ("Do you not know that the wicked will not inherit the kingdom of God?"), but I prefer justice sooner rather than later so I can reap its benefit.

Shame on me! God's patience gives people time to repent. I'm afraid by nature I'm more like Jonah, who bit-terly regretted Nineveh's repentance and resulting stay of execution from God (Jonah 4:1–3). Only the example of my Savior provides me with the motivation to aim for this unearthly level of mercy for others—he died for my sins on a cross while pleading for the forgiveness of the men who put him there.

Yes, it is quite normal to need help in resolving con-flicts! Peace and love come as the result of our humility in seeking resolution. What a blessing that God is willing to involve himself in this process though his Spirit, his word and his people. And inevitably, as we work through the most difficult conflicts in a godly way, we will learn les-sons to add to our beggar's purses that otherwise might have eluded us for a lifetime. .

23

SUBMISSION

Like many of the character traits to which God calls me, I find submission beautiful in concept and often onerous in practice. How does my sinful nature resist submission? Let me count the ways! I am prideful, willful, selfish, independent and have an over-developed, self-constructed definition of "fairness." If it were not for the Bible calling me to this attribute, it would never enter my mind, much less my behavior!

For me submission falls clearly into the category of sin Paul addressed in Romans 7:7: "I would not have known what sin was except through the law."

But for the Bible, I'd have been yet another angry feminist, raging against inequality and labeling the apostle Paul a woman-hater. However, since for most of my life I've believed the Bible to be inspired by God (2 Timothy 3:16–17 and 2 Peter 1:20–21), I'm confident God was speaking through Paul, and I am hesitant to bring charges of discrimination (or any other crime) against the Creator of the universe. My respect for God has always made me hesitant to rail against his commands. Ironically, while I refuse to argue with *God* about submission, it hasn't always kept me from arguing with Ron about it!

Most helpful to me in my quest to become a gentle, cooperative, humble person is, not surprisingly, the example of Jesus. When I contemplate the way in which he powerfully rose above the desire of his flesh to avoid the pain and humiliation of the cross, submitting both to his Father's will and to my desperate need, I am astounded at the strength and beauty of submission (Matthew 26:36–46; Philippians 2:5–11).

Maintaining this view of submission is no simple matter since my natural desires and my errant emotions war against it. Deep in my nature is an urge to have my own way, to even every score, and to have my opinions rule the day. I could give you a handful of examples, most of them petty, none of them pretty, but I'll be selective and just give one.

Many years ago, I received a small inheritance from my father. This little windfall arrived in monthly checks usually varying between $30 and $200. It came at a time when our budget was quite stretched—our oldest two kids were off to college. I very much wanted this money for my own little slush fund. Ron very much felt it needed to go into the common pot of our budget to meet everyday expenses. More than greed was involved in my desire; I had an emotional bond to these funds as a personal gift from my father, and I didn't want to share. We argued, I wept, I got advice and was counseled not to be selfish and to submit to Ron and our family's needs. I had to wrestle my sinful nature to the ground, pummel it soundly and repeatedly in order to get happy with this circumstance. My definition of "fairness" had to be re-evaluated.

I am enthralled by the power of Jesus to submit. I find the juxtaposition of roles played by Jesus and his mom at the wedding at Cana in Galilee a fascinating and helpful study in submission (John 2:1–11). There was surely an appropriate call for submission on both their parts. After all, a son should submit to his mother. On the other hand, Jesus was God in the flesh—who could be more worthy of deference?

As the scene played out, good-hearted Mary became concerned about her friends being embarrassed by running out of wine for their guests. Now, Jesus had never performed a miracle before, so it is unclear how Mary expected him to resolve this problem. Did she want him to run home to retrieve a supply from their own stash? Hop over to the local winery? Suggest the guests head on home? But she laid the problem at his feet anyway. She was honest about her feelings of concern. Jesus replied that it was neither his nor her responsibility (I can hear Ron's voice here), and that the timing was inappropriate.

Jesus, along with his Father, had apparently calculated the timing of calling attention to himself through miracles. The evidence of his deity was a factor in riling up his enemies and hastening his death. His miracles certainly turned the spotlight on him. Add to this the fact that his other miracles to follow were benevolent at a much higher level than providing wine for people who had already had enough—he healed the sick, made the lame walk, caused the blind to see, and raised the dead! Turning water into wine was a pretty shoddy introductory miracle. But Mary couldn't have known all this. All Jesus told her was that his "time [had] not yet come."

She could have submitted to his judgment on the matter. Perhaps she should have. But it was Jesus who chose to submit to her. I find this extraordinary. He was the one who was right! The timing was bad. It was not their responsibility. It was a bad idea, however well-intentioned! But it was my Lord who submitted.

Ron used to have this thing about not wanting to get into a bed that had not been crisply made up. There have been a few occasions over the years when I have neglected this chore all day long. I remember Ron asking me to make the bed at bedtime. (We've both changed over the years: Now I rarely leave the bed unmade; *he's* as likely to make it up as I am.) His end-of-the-day request annoyed me on several levels. First, I thought it was silly to make the bed just to pull the covers back and get into it. Second, I thought if he wanted it made, he should do it.

Stuffing these irritable feelings to avoid late-night conflict, I would huffily and half-heartedly yank the covers up into some semblance of order. Far be it from me to be meticulous about responding to an unreasonable (by my estimation) request!

Here's where I'm different from Jesus. He didn't want to do it. It was unwise to do it. He openly communicated his reasoning on the issue. Then he submitted and produced the best wine anyone had ever tasted! There was nothing reluctant or half-hearted or passive-aggressive about his submission. He did the very best he could.

I don't know what heavenly strategies had to be employed to stave off any bad results from this untimely miracle and to protect the overall scheme of Jesus' purposes here on earth. Nevertheless, it was his compassion and strength that won the day.

I'm dazzled! I love his self-control, his generosity, his honesty and his humility. This is the beauty of submission. This is the character I aim for.

24

THEME SONGS

You know how you'll hear a song and think, "Wow! That song resonates so deeply with me it could have been written to describe my life! Some lyricist has been spying on me and taking notes!" This is how lovers choose the melodies that they refer to as "our song."

Early on in my wild infatuation with Ron, the handsome and witty young school teacher with the smooth and beguiling southern drawl, there was a popular song on the radio called "Teacher's Pet." While I was never a student in his classroom, this song naturally caught my attention. Fifty years later, I can still sing it word for word and recapture some of the rapturous glow it originally evoked.

In films, theme songs are designed to enhance the emotional tenor of a movie and more deeply involve the viewer in the experience of the plot. They serve as a melodic summary of the storyline.

Our memories of different seasons of our lives can often be epitomized by the emotions they originally evoked. Periods of bliss or grief, exuberance or despair define our past experiences. They can also shape our future responses.

I don't know how it started. We weren't looking ahead with a plan to create a tradition associated with the hardest times of our life together. Yet, over the years, Ron and I have developed a habit of selecting theme scriptures when we are going through a trial. Some people may need a new scripture or big chunks of scripture every day to make it faithfully through hard times. Ron and I seem to need one scripture to be an anchor that we return to daily to steady us in a storm. That's not to say it's the only scripture we read on those tough days, but it is the one encapsulating an attitude we are aiming for or a reassurance we need to stake our faith on. Let me take you with me on a journey back through the hardest times of our lives.

In 1973, I was twenty-eight years old and a busy wife and mother. I had two children in elementary school and two still at home; the youngest was six months old. I began experiencing severe pain and weakness in my hands. It would wake me many times through the night and inhibit the efficiency of my days. I couldn't wring out washcloths or fasten the tiny buttons on my baby's clothes.

As I made the rounds of doctors with varying medical

specialties, my symptoms became more acute and wide-spread. By the time a rheumatologist diagnosed me with rheumatoid arthritis, my presenting symptoms were so severe that he predicted I would soon be confined to a wheelchair. I did not take this news well.

I was furious with God. I railed at him: "You've given me a family to take care of, and now you are taking away my ability to do that!" It is the only time in my life that I remember cursing in a prayer, referring to "this #*!!**// arthritis."

Eventually, I realized I needed to surrender to a future that might not look like the one I had envisioned for myself and accept the future God had planned. I admitted to God that I could still be used by him from a wheel chair, just not in the way I had always dreamed I would be. I gave up my dreams and embraced whatever his dreams for me might be.

The verse I clung to during this time was Jeremiah 29:11: "For I know the plans I have for you, plans to prosper you and not to harm you." I acknowledged that there is a difference between hurt and harm, and fixed my hope on ways God could use me in spite of my new limitations.

Within months of this surrender, I went into remission. I don't try to interpret this blessing (I don't believe my surrender was some sort of bartering chip with God that once displayed caused him to heal me), but I accept it with gratitude along with the lessons I learned from the experience.

In 1982, Ron was diagnosed with cancer. We were shocked and frightened. An early uncertain prognosis left us emotionally frayed. We settled on James 4:13–15 as our theme:

> Now listen, you who say, "Today or tomorrow we will go to this or that city, spend a year there, carry on business and make money." Why, you do not even know what will happen tomorrow. What is your life? You are a mist that appears for a little while and then vanishes. Instead, you ought to say, "If it is the Lord's will, we will live and do this or that."

We only knew how to cope with one day at a time. We had to leave our future in the hands of a God who knows all. We had to relinquish a quest for control over our lives. We tried to live righteously in the face of each day's circumstances.

This settling perspective came from a focus on living one day at a time. It was hard work and against our natures, but it kept our heads above water emotionally and spiritually. It provided a lesson that has carried us through many other trials.

We were frightened to learn in 1995 that Ron would

need triple bypass surgery. In facing that scary operation and recovery, Ron found confidence in Psalm 73:26:

> My flesh and my heart may fail,
>> but God is the strength of my heart and my por-
>> tion forever.

As Ron shared this scripture with me, it became my source of comfort as well. Our security is in the forever provisions of God, not in our ability to manipulate our certain mortality.

On the few occasions that one or another of our children have gone through spiritual struggles, I have found that my best focus is Romans 12:12: "Be joyful in hope, patient in affliction, faithful in prayer." I am most vulnerable to panic and despair and a temptation to be controlling when I fear my child is walking away from God. This is very inappropriate now that they are all adults. A very wise friend once told me, "When you can't find joy in your present circumstances, be joyful in hope."

This resonated with me deeply. Still, I had to come to terms with what to hope for. That may sound silly to you, but I struggle with trying to figure out exactly how God will work in a situation, and I want him to hurry. With focused effort now I try to trust God with the details and just ask for his intervention, omitting my suggestions about the how and when.

While my mother was struggling with the horrible symptoms of Alzheimer's disease, I was struggling with a grief process that consumed me. As I watched my friends, Shanti and Lena, love and serve my mom with joy, they helped me see that I needed to rise above my own sorrow to become what Mom needed. My mantra came from Romans 12:8: Use your gift in proportion to your faith. "If it is showing mercy, let him do it cheerfully." My efforts at showing mercy to my mom were far from cheerful.

While Alzheimer's patients have limitations in what they can conceive and retain, they remain in tune with the emotional climate around them. Mom was best served by my joy. She had no way of understanding or responding to my sorrow except to mirror it. Her best hope of joy was the cheerful attitude I (and others) could offer her.

I had to consciously set aside my own feelings and capture a detached sweetness to be what she needed. This was no small task on my part and probably could not have been accomplished without the example of my faithful friends to imitate and a daily return to my goal scripture, "...do it cheerfully."

In my experience, I sometimes have been unable to change a behavior or attitude until I gained a clear picture of what I was aiming for. Then I could make some progress, however slowly and painfully, toward a godlier attitude.

When an x-ray revealed an 8cm. mass in my left lung in 2006, pathology reports determined that I had an unusual presentation of non-Hodgkin's lymphoma. It is incurable, but treatable, and the prognosis is uncertain because no studies have been done on this disease when it grows in lymphatic tissue as opposed to lymph nodes.

My theme scripture has been Job 12:10: "In his hand is the life of every creature and the breath of all mankind." This is most comforting because my breathing has definitely been compromised. Labored breathing, while not a constant state, is not my favorite thing. It just makes me very happy to know that while doctors are limited in their knowledge and resources, God is not, and he has a perfect plan.

The challenge for me now is to be responsible with my health without being consumed; cautious about exposure to infections without becoming paranoid; laughing without escaping into denial; and open without complaining. I don't know how to walk this unfamiliar path, but I can see some progress I've made in waiting on the Lord.

A theme is something that summarizes a story. A theme captures the essence of the meaning assigned to any given circumstance or, in a written work, sets forth the topic to be enlarged upon.

I want my life's theme to be the faith with which I approach trials, not the trials themselves. I don't want to be defined by circumstances, good or bad. David wrote in Psalm 119:54, "Your decrees are the theme of my song…." I long for my faith to be a theme that overshadows and conquers every other attitude, the primary melody to which every other voice submits in harmonious deference.

THOUGHTS FROM THE AUTHOR

We all come to God as beggars if we approach him understanding our true position before him. The wonderful assurance is that we do not come to a reluctant benefactor, but to a Father eager to give us "...everything we need for life and godliness..." (2 Peter 1:3).

It is good from time to time to sort through the lessons and gifts (such as answered prayers) accumulated in your beggar's purse. Reflecting upon the amazing faithfulness of God can renew your gratitude and reconfirm your determination to persevere. It can show you how far you've come in your spiritual growth, which is especially helpful if you are the type to become easily discouraged with yourself.

My highest goal in writing this book was to be vulnerable with my own life and struggles, and to point my reader to the loving God who has put up with me, blessed me and changed me. In this ongoing process of life-change, I find great encouragement in reflecting on how patient God has always been with me. I hope that as you read through this little spiritual memoir, you were encouraged, too.

Other Writings

The following writings are chapters I wrote in several anthologies published by DPI. I offer these as added resources and encouraging helps. Note that the publication date of these chapters was several years ago, so some of the life facts reflect this difference.

Godly Emotions
Life and Godliness for Everywoman: Volume One

Picture Satan looking on at creation—hating God's success and achievement—tense, frightened, hateful, plotting…

God: Let there be light!
Satan: I will bring such a permeating darkness that it will overcome your light!

God: Let there be sky and clouds, oceans and rivers. Add some continents with mountains, and canyons and prairies and deserts! Now let us have some trees and flowers, fruits and vegetables, and bushes and vines—everything from cactus to tropical forests!
Satan: "I'll pollute and destroy it!

Just Like Me

> Then God said, "Let us make man in our image, in our likeness, and let them rule over the fish of the sea and the birds of the air, over the livestock, over all the earth, and over all the creatures that move along the ground." (Genesis 1:26)

We cannot fathom how many dreams God invested in the statement, "Let us make man in our image, and in our likeness…." He doesn't want our hairlines and noses to resemble his! He wants our characters, our choices and our values to resemble his. He wants us to feel the same way about things that he feels (Romans 12:9) and take action accordingly! Consider the following interaction:

God: I will give her freedom of choice—I don't want robots.

Satan: Perfect! I will arrange a myriad of appealing choices.

God: I will make her creative.

Satan: I will make her lazy so she'll waste her talents. Failing that, I'll make her competitive, greedy and materialistic.

God: I will give her emotion and the ability to care.

Satan: I will shut her down or make her a victim of her emotions.

God: I will give her love.

Satan: I will help her love herself.

God: I will give her joy.

Satan: I will make her a pleasure-seeker.

God: I will give her sorrow so she can weep with those who weep.

Satan: I will teach her self-pity.

God: I will give her the ability to hate—so that she can hate evil.

Satan: I will make her hate her brother and sometimes even God.

God: I will give her a capacity for righteous anger.

Satan: I will teach her fits of rage.

God: I will give her a conscience so she can feel remorse for sin.

Satan: I will put her on guilt-trips, so that instead of being motivated by guilt, she'll be paralyzed by it.

God: I will give her a holy, protective fear.

Satan: I will teach her hysterical fear.

God: I will give her zeal.

Satan: I will give her worldly causes to capture her zeal.

God: I will give her enthusiasm and exuberance.

Satan: I will make her crave excitement, and I will give her an insatiable hunger for the fantasies of lust and the high of intoxication.

God: I will give her gratitude.

Satan: I will teach her to take things for granted and to expect more.

Fallen

Oh, this little fantasized list could be so much longer! I'm sure you can think of so many other characteristics and emotions that God meant for good and that Satan destroys or distorts in our lives.

When mankind fell in the Garden of Eden, his and her emotions took a fall as well. By nature, I am melancholy and moody, prone to fretting and hysteria. I sound like a real fun person to be around, don't I? Until I had a relationship with God, I had nothing to help me keep these tendencies in check apart from social graces. On occasion I was a nice person. But the people I lived with saw the unrestrained me.

Why do we sometimes say and believe: "I can't help the way I feel"? If it were true that we have no control over our emotions, God would never have commanded us to love (Ephesians 5:1) or rejoice (Philippians 4:4) or mourn (Romans 12:15).

I remember having bouts of PMS or postpartum blues and thinking, *Surely the Holy Spirit is stronger than my hormones! Why can't I shake this?* I even wondered if hormone possession is the same as demon possession. My husband wondered too! The Bible makes it clear that Satan has access to our circumstances. (Review the conversation between God and Satan about Job.) Experience suggests to me that he has the access code to our moods as well.

In Good Company

Fortunately, the Bible doesn't leave us with the illusion that its heroes had no emotional struggles! I shudder to think how some of us might have counseled Jeremiah if he had taken his emotional outburst to them instead of to God. (And God even saw fit to print it for posterity without a qualifying rebuke.) Read through Jeremiah 20:7–18, and think of the counsel Jeremiah might have gotten from a well-meaning, godly friend today.

Jeremiah accuses and insults God. He seems full of self-pity and paranoia. He blames God and curses his mother for giving him birth. By today's standards, we would say he was schizophrenic, bipolar or at least temporarily irrational. I think Jeremiah would have cried out: *No! These are not things I mean! These are things I feel! I don't know how else to express the agony and confusion inside me.*

Jeremiah did two significant things: (1) he prayed and (2) he was totally honest in his prayers. Polite prayers will never lance the infected boils in our hearts. There is no point in it anyway! God knows what is really in there better than we do. Sometimes we take our hysteria to half a dozen people before we take it to God. I'm not saying we should not be open with and gain perspective from the people God has put in our lives, but we need to take prayer to a deeper and more honest level with God!

I think it was that tubby philosopher, Winnie the Pooh, who said: "How can I know what I think until it is out in the air where I can look at it?" It's very true that just by putting our feelings into words, we become more objective about them. Unspoken, negative feelings fester and sometimes take on a life of their own. We should never trust our emotions until we pray about them and express them to a godly, objective person.

We can't know what we ought to feel until we know the heart of God! Most of humanity is subject to the emotions that come most naturally to their temperaments and their circumstances. Animals are guided by instinct and temperament. But we are made in the image of God, and therefore, we can be *in control of* our emotions rather than *being controlled by* them. In Ephesians 4:26 God instructs us: "In your anger, do not sin." There are many sinful ways to express anger. We can choose to be "slow to become angry" (James 1:19). We can choose to "speak the truth in love" (Ephesians 4:15).

Be Open

Jesus is clearly the best example of how to work through intense emotions so that they do not control our behavior (Matthew 26:36–56). While at Gethsemane, he was open with his closest friends. He was also honest with his emotions in prayer. He kept praying until he found peace in the circumstances facing him.

The apostle Paul is another great example of rising above circumstances to remain content and joyful. Paul wrote the book of Philippians from a prison cell. His sentence was unjust, and people who should have been compassionate and supportive were spiteful. Still, Paul talks repeatedly of his joy and gratitude. He found the "up" side of everything! He saw his imprisonment as a blessing because it had allowed him to preach to the whole palace guard (1:12–14). Although some preachers on the outside were trying to hurt him, he was just glad they were still preaching about Jesus! (1:15–18). He stayed

- hopeful (1:19)
- confident (1:25–26)
- Christ-focused (2:5–11)
- indifferent to personal suffering (2:17)
- others-centered (2:19–30)
- patient (3:1)
- spiritual and humble (3:2–11)
- goal-oriented (3:12–16).

Then he asked us to follow his example (3:17).

Paul doesn't feign perfection. He tells us not to be anxious and gives us a great formula for dealing with anxiety in Philippians 4:4–9: Pray about your concerns, stay grateful, keep focused on the positive and imitate him. He also felt anxiety (Philippians 2:28) but he tells us that he had learned the "secret of being content in any and every situation." His contentment came through God.

Make a Decision

One thing is clear throughout this remarkable book. Paul's joy was in God alone! As long as Paul knew God was in control, that the gospel was still being preached and heaven was still his destination—he was happy. Paul had decided what the source of his happiness would be. Life will have its ups and downs. Hormones will ebb and flow. Temperaments will still be genetically influenced. But surer and greater than all these things are God and his promises. Have you *decided* what the source of your happiness will be?

When your joy fades, can you recapture it with prayer, openness, godly advice and gratitude? You can. I can. We can if we decide that God is enough for happiness, whether or not we have anything else in the world. Decide what the source of your happiness will be.

Go to War

This is not an automatic ticket back to the land of the

problem-free happies! It is not a pat answer. It is a formula for regaining perspective so that in the middle of the most overwhelming tugs on our emotions, we have something we can do to keep from basing our decisions on those emotions. It takes hard work. It takes making every effort! Negative emotions sap you of your energy, so just when you need the most energy, you have the least. That is where God comes in! "I can do everything through him who gives me strength" (Philippians 4:13).

Do not feel guilty about prolonged sadness. Get help. If you add guilt to a heart already overcome with negative emotions, you start feeling hopeless. There are certainly times when a trained professional and possibly anti-depressants are needed. I am not talking about those times.

I remember a time when circumstances had brought me so low, the only scripture that I could identify with was Psalm 88. I thought, *Wow! I'm in the Bible! The chapter ends without telling me how to get out of this place, but at least it lets me know God understands how I feel—and for some reason, he chose to put it in the Bible!*

One of the things I learned during that time was that you can feel more than one thing at a time! You can feel joy and sorrow at the same time. You may not be able to decide which feeling you wake up with, but with *much effort*, you can decide which feeling will determine your actions through that day. You can decide whether you will dwell on the negative or on the positive. That is called "taking every thought captive" (2 Corinthians 10:5). It sounds like war and struggle, doesn't it? Well, that is what it takes!

I read an article once that said to overcome or ward off depression, every day you should

- Get enough sleep
- Eat regular, well-balanced meals
- Get some aerobic exercise
- Get at least half an hour of *positive* social interaction (this cannot include talking to someone about your problems because they are negative)
- Get an hour alone
- Spend time in meditation, prayer or whatever feeds your spiritual side
- Finish at least one task, so that you have a sense of accomplishment at the end of every day
- Laugh or sing

"Rejoice in the Lord!" When you can't rejoice in circumstances, rejoice in the Lord. When you can't rejoice in health or being pain-free, rejoice in the Lord. When you can't rejoice in an absence of conflict, rejoice in the Lord.

When God is factored into the equation, there's always hope. The bleakest outlook can be changed with hope. Don't let Satan carry out his schemes of controlling you with negative emotions. Go to battle and defeat him with your hope and joy!

Sheila Jones, ed. *Life and Godliness for Everywoman, Volume 1* (Spring Hill, TN: DPI, 2001). The book is available from DPI.

EVE
The Great Deception
She Shall Be Called Woman: Volume One

Genesis 2, 3, 4; 2 Corinthians 11:3; 1 Timothy 2:13

Eve's history in a word is God. A split second before the world came into being, there was God—God with an idea that only he could bring to fruition. A world with color. Design. Detail. Incredibly delicate balances. And in the middle of it all, man and woman—made to be the objects of his love, to be the reflection of his nature, to be the recipients of his care. The Divine fashions and then holds the hand of mankind. Now mankind must decide if he and she will be led or will let loose.

The Garden of Eden. Perfection. Unspeakable beauty. The presence of God. Can you imagine it? Unbroken union with the Creator! Walking with him, talking with him, learning from him, loving and being loved by him! The God who created Adam and Eve in perfection built into them the capacity for choice. Without the power to choose, there would have been no relationship. They would have been nothing more than robots. But if they chose to love God, chose to trust him, chose to obey him, they would hold on to perfection. God made choice viable by placing a forbidden tree in the garden and giving them the option of trust or doubt, obedience or rebellion. With choice came the possibility of deception.

We can better understand how sin's deception works in our lives if we understand how Satan deceived Eve. To look at Eve is to see ourselves. God has a continuing concern for his people in every century, "...I am afraid that just as Eve was deceived by the serpent's cunning, your minds may somehow be led astray from your sincere and pure devotion to Christ" (2 Corinthians 11:3–4). How did Satan lead Eve astray?

The Deception of Doubt

Eve had never seen anything but perfection. Unblemished goodness enveloped and permeated her life. There had been no negative circumstances to cause her to doubt or question God. His goodness, faithfulness, power and love had been shown in every way. She had never been given one reason to suspect that God would withhold anything wonderful from her. She had never experienced sickness, pain, grief, betrayal, war or natural calamity. She had never had an unmet need, a sleepless night or an unanswered prayer. Yet, at Satan's first suggestion that God lacked integrity toward her, Eve entertained doubts!

- Maybe I am missing something heady and intriguing.
- Maybe God is selfishly hoarding a blessing I would really enjoy.
- Maybe he didn't *really* mean what he said.
- Maybe he makes idle threats.
- Maybe he doesn't really have my best interest at heart.

We tend to feel that life's negative circumstances justify our questioning God's benevolence towards us. We get angry at God. Eve's story reveals that it is not our circumstances that make us question God—it is the sinful nature. That is why people with pure hearts grow closer to God in adversity, and those with doubting hearts turn away from God.

The Deception of Desire

The lusts of her flesh blocked her reason. Satan convinced her that she could fulfill her desires and suffer no consequences. *"You will surely not die."* It looked good. It smelled good. It tasted good. It sounded good. She was afraid to miss out. She was curious, restless, feeling unfulfilled. She would be the exception. She would get away with it. Just this one time. Like us: I won't get pregnant. I won't get a sexually transmitted disease, suffer the addiction, the overdose, the breakdown. I won't be charged with drunk driving. Those things happen to other people.

When we are ungrateful for what we do have, we desire what we should not have. The fruit—Eve wanted its beauty, flavor and power. She wanted the knowledge of good and evil. She already had the knowledge of good; for the first, last and only time in history, human beings experienced perfect good! But she was not able to appreciate it until she had experienced evil, and then it was too late— for all of us!

What must this grieving mother have thought as she stood weeping over the grave of her son, Abel, senselessly murdered by his brother, Cain, knowing that she had wanted the knowledge of good and evil? In essence, she had asked to witness this shameful horror! Satan must have been delighted. You want to see evil? I will show you evil! And with the permission of our own sinfully curious natures, Satan continues to show us evil—tragic, chaotic, destructive evil.

The Deception of Distance

I wonder where Eve thought God was while she carried on this little chat with Satan and wiped the fruit juice off her chin with the back of her hand? She was like the prodigal son who "set off for a distant country" and there squandered his wealth in wild living. In senseless denial, Eve distanced herself from an all-seeing God. Then upon hearing him approach, she pathetically attempted to hide.

We distance ourselves with self-deception. God appeals to us not to kid ourselves about sin and its consequences (Galatians 6:7–8; James 1:16–17, 22–27). What lies did Eve tell herself to blur the clarity of God's instructions: "You are free to eat from any tree in the garden; but you must not eat from the tree of the knowledge of good and evil, for when you eat of it you will surely die" (Genesis 2:16–17)? We feel insulted when we become victims of someone else's lies—how much more insulting it is to become victims of our lies to ourselves! That's what happens when mind games shut out reality. Fantasy convinces us that everything will be all right in spite of our sin. We misinterpret God's grace to mean that he will sweep sin under the rug (Romans 6).

We distance ourselves not only from the reality of God's presence, but also from his clear and perfect standard. We back away from that standard as we interpret, rationalize, minimize and blame shift. Eve used all of these techniques when she answered God's question, *"What is this that you have done?"* Her rationalized, minimized, blame shifted response was, *"The serpent deceived me and I ate."*

We cannot slip things past God. But our natures long to believe the deception that a sin is too small, too brief, too unavoidable or too long ago for God to have noticed or remembered. And, just as he asked Eve, God asks us, "Where are you?" He asks, not because he does not know, but because he wants to give us an opportunity to admit where we are and to come back to him.

Grateful or Doubtful?

Like Eve's, my life is filled with evidence of God's faithfulness, but by nature I am not a grateful person. Although I have grown to be more focused on solutions than on problems, I still sometimes fail the tests and give way to worry or doubt.

Years ago our youngest son, Matt (then twenty years old and a college junior), left Chicago for Syracuse, New York, to be part of a new church. He was full of dreams to do great things for God. There were blessings on every hand: He loved the church, his friends, his classes and his job. But there was something in the air in Syracuse that caused Matt to have daily asthma attacks. By September his condition was life-threatening. Prolonged, acute coughing had perforated both his lungs. In October he finally realized he would have to leave in order to get well.

Satan was right there, urging me to be faithless and fearful. He whispered, sometimes shouted, doubt-provoking questions in my ears:

- Maybe he never should have gone to Syracuse in the first place.
- Maybe irreparable damage has been done to his lungs, and he'll be sickly for the rest of his life.
- What an expensive waste to have to drop his classes mid-semester!
- What if he gets discouraged about losing a year and doesn't go back to school?
- Why would God give him the best friends, job and classes he's ever had and then take it away so quickly?
- Why this?
- Why that?
- Why something else?
- I have a right to worry. After all, I *am* his mother.

Stop it, Satan!

When I stayed in touch with my profound gratitude to God for his faithfulness to Matt throughout his life, for the people God had surrounded him with, for the lessons that are only learned through trials, I was able to gain perspective. There was no reason to believe that God would suddenly stop blessing and directing Matt's life or that this illness was an interruption to God's plan. Hope. Peace. Joyful expectation. What's next, Father?

Matt eventually moved to Los Angeles, healthy, happy, eager to get back into school, spiritually growing and eager. God proved his faithfulness. My constant challenge in the face of trials is to refuse to entertain doubts. Staying focused on the abundant evidence of God's love and faithfulness is what will keep me deaf to the doubts Satan lays before me—and worry *is* doubt.

When Eve became ungrateful for what she had, she was easy prey for the deception of doubt. We tend to take for granted whatever blessings we are used to, even perfection, if we have nothing with which to compare it! Gratitude is the essential element of living a faithful, doubt-free life!

Focus Questions

What problems can tempt you to lose a grateful focus on God's blessings in your life and cause you to worry or doubt?

Do you spend more time focused on problems or solutions, fears or faith?

Linda Brumley and Sheila Jones, eds. *She Shall Be Called Woman, Vol 1, Second Edition, Old Testament Women* (Spring Hill, TN: DPI, 1998). This book is available from DPI along with volume 2 (*New Testament Women*).

JOANNA
A Gutsy Follower
She Shall Be Called Woman: Volume Two

Luke 8:1–3; 23:49, 55–56; 24:1–12

A carpenter's son from Nazareth was roaming the countryside on foot, attracting crowds wherever he went. His teachings were compelling, insightful and authoritative. He often taught in parables and quoted knowledgeably from the Scriptures. He never backed off from a challenging question and never lost a debate. And if there was any chance that he might be dismissed as just another philosopher, he performed miracle after miracle to confirm that his message had a divine source.

Gravity was defied, winds were calmed, and waves were stilled. The lame were healed, the blind were given sight, lepers were cleansed, the dead were raised, and demons lost their battles before a superior power. Some of those healed he allowed to accompany him; others he sent back to their homes. Some he encouraged to share their stories, others he charged to tell no one. His fame spread widely. Even those who had never met him had opinions about him because of the things they had heard.

Herod the tetrarch himself was curious and hoped to meet him someday. That meeting would finally occur on the day Pilate sent Jesus to be tried before Herod. But two or three years prior to that trial, could it be that Herod's curiosity was first piqued by the wife of one of his own servants?

She is only mentioned twice and only in the book of Luke. Someone once observed that the Holy Spirit does not waste ink. There are important lessons to be learned from Joanna. Otherwise God would not have included her name in the story of his Son.

When we first meet Joanna in Luke 8, we find her in a very elite group. She numbered among a few women who accompanied Jesus and the Twelve, traveling with them from town to town. She had been profoundly affected by him, having been healed of either a physical malady or demon-possession. She had heard the parables and witnessed the miracles.

She was married. Her husband, Cuza, was employed by Herod Antipas, tetrarch of Galilee, but often referred to as *king*—one of the more prominent and powerful enemies of the man she loved and followed (Luke 13:31). She had some money of her own, and she gave it to Jesus for his ministry and support. Her loyalty to a controversial trouble-maker was probably awkward for her husband. His boss's father had tried to kill the child Jesus (Matthew 2:13–20), and now it was Herod's kingship that was threatened by this new "King of the Jews."

Many pressures could have worn her down and caused her to give up on the initial exuberant gratitude that made her risk so much to follow Jesus. But she stuck with him until the very end. She was in the crowd that heard the parable of the sower (Luke 8:4–15), and perhaps when Jesus talked about the seed springing up quickly with joy, she thought of her own conversion. When he warned of falling away because of a lack of roots, perhaps it produced in her a conviction to make her roots go deep enough to withstand the tests that life would surely bring.

The Test of Perseverance

It is hard to imagine, considering her husband's career, that he would be very supportive of his wife's faith, especially considering her visibility, the time commitment and the financial implications. I can hear his tirades: "You are making me look like a fool. You are a threat to my job. I thought you believed in submission." It is speculation, of course, but I suspect she faced opposition from many sources.

I often think of seeing her in heaven someday. I have

so many questions to ask to fill in the gaps from Luke 8 to Luke 24. In the latter, she is mentioned as "Joanna," not "Joanna, the wife of Cuza." Maybe it doesn't mean anything at all. Or maybe it does. Maybe he died. And then, maybe he divorced her when he forced her to choose between Jesus and him, and she chose Jesus. Maybe Herod pressured Cuza. At any rate, I wish Luke 24 could read, "Joanna and Cuza, former manager of Herod's household, returned from the empty tomb...."

Whatever the events of those intense years, she persevered through the bright times and the dark times, hanging on to a commitment that saw her through to the very end. I long for the time when I can sit at her feet and hear her story and tell her how much I admired her even from the little I knew.

The Test of Heartbreak

She was, no doubt, among "the women who followed him from Galilee, [who] stood at a distance, watching [the crucifixion]" (Luke 23:49). She must have followed Joseph of Arimathea after he claimed the battered body and took it to the tomb (Luke 23:55). She was probably up all night with the other women preparing the spices and perfumes as a final tender service to the man they had adored. It was certainly a unique girls' night out—subdued conversation, busy hands, questions, memories, tears, smiles, shattered dreams, uncertain hope. It must have been an uneasy rest that Sabbath while they waited to visit the tomb on Sunday.

The Test of Danger

She surely understood the danger of displaying her loyalty to this rebel at his execution. The men definitely understood. Peter denied Jesus three times, while the rest deserted him and went into hiding. They did not risk visiting the tomb until the guards were gone—since no corpse was left to guard. Perhaps it was an advantage being a woman. Perhaps they were considered no serious threat in that culture; insignificant and sentimental, they were free to go through their little rituals of grief and be done with it.

Nevertheless, I am inspired by Joanna and the other women who risked the danger of association with an executed criminal. Their love and gratitude produced a faith and courage that enabled them to be loyal against all odds.

The Test of Disrespect

Sometimes the people who ought to offer the greatest encouragement and support will disappoint you.

...Joanna and the others...told this [the empty tomb report] to the apostles. But they did not believe the women because their words seemed to them like nonsense. (Luke 24:10–11)

What an insult! Of all the people who should have believed them, the apostles topped the list. But the other victories of her faith make me confident that she rose above her pride to avoid the temptation of a spiteful, critical nature that might have said, "How dare these self-righteous cowards dismiss us so glibly. We are eyewitnesses, and we know we are right!"

She remembered, I am sure, Jesus' words: "Forgive and you will be forgiven...Why do you look at the speck in your brother's eye and pay no attention to the plank in your own eye?" (Luke 6:37–42). She doesn't seem like a woman who would pass every other test and then give in to pettiness.

Joanna, a loyal friend and follower of Jesus. He turned her life and her world upside down, and she refused to allow anyone to turn it back.

Enduring Gratitude

I am challenged most by the gratitude in Joanna's life that produced her perseverance. She was saved from not only a specific ailment, but more importantly, from spiritual death. My gratitude for what I have been saved from should motivate a faith, love and courage great enough to make me persevere through any test. I never want to forget what I would be like without Jesus, and I want that to be the motivating force in my life to the very end.

I used to read Titus 2:3 ("Likewise, teach the older women to be reverent in the way they live, not to be slanderers or addicted to much wine, but to teach what is good.") and wonder why older women would be vulnerable to an addiction to wine. Living now in my fifth decade, I have a hunch that addiction to wine was the retirement mentality of the first century: a little relaxation, a little escape from responsibility, a little edge off the aches and pains.

My zeal is no longer fed by youthful energy. The zeal for living a reverent, productive life has to come from a deeper source of conviction, gratitude and love that must be renewed daily. I realized recently that I had grown tired and dull. A combination of circumstances, including recurring fatigue (a symptom of my rheumatoid arthritis) had tested me, and I had failed the test. I pushed through the routines of my days attending to the most visible demands. I did not think through my priorities and the efficient use of the energy I *did* have. I did not apply my creativity to make things work. *Everything* had grown dull—my quiet times, my discipline, my evangelism.

A single lesson at a midweek service became my wake-up call from God. It was hard getting focused again to prioritize my days and delegate the tasks better done by someone else. It was harder still to eliminate some activities that were non-productive. Those hard changes probably would have been impossible to make without the helpful input of an objective friend. I desperately needed someone else's spiritual perspective.

Repentance is sweet, and I saw God's blessings immediately, including a sense of increased energy as I felt more fulfillment from being more productive. James 1:3 says that perseverance is produced by the testing of your faith. In addition, it is *motivated* by gratitude and love and is *encouraged* by discipline.

Focus Question

How high is your gratitude level?

Does it motivate you to persevere?

Linda Brumley and Sheila Jones, eds. *She Shall Be Called Woman, Vol 2, Second Edition, New Testament Women* (Spring Hill, TN: DPI, 1998). This book is available from DPI along with volume 1 (*Old Testament Women*).

Wisdom for Life

Other Volumes in the Devotional Series for Women
Available from DPI

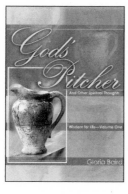

God's Pitcher
And Other Spiritual Thoughts
Gloria Baird

The first book in the Wisdom for Life series of women's devotional books features short, insightful readings. Gloria Baird shares nuggets of wisdom with which she has nurtured, counseled and encouraged women throughout the years. As God has poured into her pitcher, so has she poured into the pitchers of others.

My Bucket of Sand
And Other Spiritual Thoughts
Sheila Jones

Psalm 139 describes the thoughts of God as being more numerous than the grains of sand—vast, uncountable, unfathomable. Sheila Jones celebrates the fact that God graciously shares some of his thoughts with us, and allows us to encourage others with them. In this book, Sheila shares some of the sand God has put in her bucket.

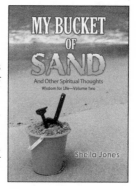